BERLITZ®

D0361363

MUNICH

11th Printing
1993/1994 Edition

Updated or revised 1992, 1991, 1988, 1986, 1985, 1984, 1982

How to use our guide

● All the practical information, hints and tips that you will need before and during the trip start on page 102.

● For general background, see the sections The City and the People, p. 6, and A Brief History, p. 12.

● All the sights to see are listed between pages 28 and 77, with suggestions on daytrips from Munich on pages 78 to 86.

    Our own choice of sights most highly recommended is pinpointed by the Berlitz traveller symbol.

● Entertainment, nightlife and all other leisure activities are described between pages 86 and 94, while information on restaurants and cuisine is to be found on pages 94 to 101.

● Finally, there is an index at the back of the book, pp. 126–127.

Found an error or an omission in this Berlitz Guide? Or a change or new feature we should know about? Our editor would be happy to hear from you, and a postcard would do. Be sure to include your name and address, since in appreciation for a useful suggestion, we'd like to send you a free travel guide. Write to: Berlitz Publishing Co. Ltd., Berlitz House, Peterley Road, Horspath, Oxford OX4 2TX, England.

Although we make every effort to ensure the accuracy of all the information in this book, changes occur incessantly. We cannot therefore take responsibility for facts, prices, addresses and circumstances in general that are constantly subject to alteration.

Text: Jack Altman
Photography: Eric Jaquier; cover picture, Georg Stärk
Layout: Doris Haldemann
Staff editor: Earleen Brunner
For their help in the preparation and updating of this book, we wish to thank Mechthild Meyer-Schneidewind, Karin Goedecke, Barbara Lerch, Seán Adamson. We are also very grateful to the German National Tourist Office, the Münchner Verkehrs- und Tarifverbund and Lufthansa German Airlines for their considerable assistance.
Cartography: 🔵 Falk-Verlag, Hamburg

Contents

Cover picture: Tony Stone Photolibrary – London.

The City and the People

To northerners seeking the easy, relaxed life of southern Europe, Munich seems almost Mediterranean. This last main stop before the Alps provides, for many, a first breath of Italy.

By the same token, for southern Europeans heading towards the prosperous efficiency of the cooler north, the Bavarian capital—more Baroque than Gothic, more green than grey—makes the transition less abrupt. A lot of them—Greeks, Yugoslavs, Italians—decide quite simply to stop in Munich and enjoy the best of both worlds. Munich's gain. Italians themselves claim the city has the best Italian restaurants north of the Alps.

For Munich's genius has always been its ability to combine the Germanic talent for getting things done with a specifically Bavarian need to do them pleasantly. Business lunches seem to last a little longer. Office hours seem a little shorter. Yet no one who has seen the town's impressive affluence, its dynamic car industry, brilliantly constructed Olympic sports complex and splendid underground system

would suggest that this somewhat casual attitude was unproductive.

If the people of Munich do differ so much from other Germans, that is because, you'll be told, this isn't Germany, it's Bavaria. As the capital of the fervently Catholic and conservative Free State of Bavaria, Munich epitomizes the independent Bavarian spirit. Good-natured local chauvinism knows no bounds. Whole books are filled with jokes at the expense of stiff-necked Prussians. At the city's renowned Oktoberfest, a beer festival, visitors sing *Warum ist es am Rhein so schön?* (Why is it so lovely on the Rhine?) to the great amusement of the locals who, they say, know without asking why Bavaria's so lovely.

The Oktoberfest is, perhaps, what first strikes the popular imagination in regard to Munich. Indeed, with annual consumption of 5,000,000 litres of beer by 6,500,000 visitors— including well over a million kids—it is a grandiose event appropriate to the oversized image the Bavarians have of their capital. It's also the most

Marienplatz, in front of the Town Hall—great spot for a good beer.

extravagant expression of that untranslatable German feeling of warm fellowship known as *Gemütlichkeit.*

But it would be wrong to think of life in Munich as one long Oktoberfest. After the post-war division of Berlin, Munich became the undisputed cultural capital of the Federal Republic of Germany—no mean achievement against the considerable claims of Hamburg, Frankfurt and Cologne. The opera house and concert halls make the town a musical mecca still, especially for the performance of works by Mozart, Wagner and Richard Strauss.

Painters also enjoy the favourable artistic climate, particularly in the bohemian district of Schwabing, which exploded on the international scene in the 20th century as a focus for the Blaue Reiter school of Wassily Kandinsky, Paul Klee and Franz Marc. Munich galleries are still among the most innovative, and the classical and modern collections of the Alte and Neue Pinakothek museums are richly endowed and superbly displayed.

Munich has become a centre for industry and publishing, as well as for the much-admired New German Cinema and its world-famous directors, Volker Schloendorff, Werner Herzog and Rainer Werner Fassbinder.

But we cannot forget the darker side of the city—evoked by Adolf Hitler's early association with Munich and the formation there of the Nazi Party —with all the ugliness that this entailed for the social and architectural identity of Bavaria's capital. Yet it was Munich's cultural atmosphere that originally attracted the future dictator to the city, at a time when he still dreamed of becoming a great painter. The years from 1918 to 1945 were, in the end perhaps, only a stormy political interlude for Munich, and the townspeople seem happy to relinquish the political spotlight to Bonn and Berlin.

Munich is attached to its historical identity. After the destruction of World War II, many German cities decided to break with the past and build in a completely modern style. But the Bavarian capital preferred to painstakingly restore and reconstruct the great churches and palaces of its

The kings have left the Residenz to the ordinary people of Munich.

Munich is part and parcel of its sleepy rural hinterland: churches with onion domes and cattle barns.

past. There are plenty of modern skyscrapers, but the heart of the old city has authentically recaptured its Baroque charm. Some have complained that the reconstruction and renovation have been too thorough, too "clean", but, in a couple of decades, the ravages of pollution have given the new-old buildings a patina of age that it previously took centuries to acquire. In fact, the reconstruction has been so complete and so convincing that monuments such as the Siegestor (Victory Gate) have been kept in their bomb-scarred condition as a historic warning.

The inner city is a pedestrian's delight, thanks to a clever town plan that keeps much of the traffic circling rather than crossing the city centre (except through underpasses)—and an

excellent system of public transport. Beyond the city centre, the broad, tree-lined avenues and boulevards planned by Bavaria's last kings open up the town with considerable elegance.

In the Englischer Garten, the city has a veritable jewel among Europe's great parks, immensely enhanced by the ebullient River Isar. The swiftly flowing waters are evidence of the proximity of the Alps from which the river flows.

And on clear days, the mountains seem to lie just beyond the southern suburbs. That's when the *Föhn* is blowing, the famous wind that gives some people a headache and others phenomenally clear creative insights. A characteristic Munich ambiguity.

When those mountains reappear on the city's doorstep, they remind the people of the country from which many of them or their parents first came. Every weekend there is a massive exodus to the villages and lakes around the city: east to the Chiemsee, west and south to the Ammersee, Starnberger See and Tegernsee, north to Schleissheim and Freising. Here the citizens of Munich can indulge in hiking, sailing, hunting and fishing— or visiting aunts and uncles for coffee and cakes.

In the winter, they trek further south into the surrounding mountains for skiing, an integral part of Munich life. Munich is undoubtedly a metropolis and in many ways a sophisticated one, but the city also retains a resolutely rural atmosphere, never losing sight of its origins in the peasant hinterland. Visitors would be wrong not to participate in Munich's happy mixture of town and country. **11**

A Brief History

Munich arrived late on the Bavarian scene. In the Middle Ages, at a time when Nuremberg, Augsburg and Regensburg were already thriving cities, the present-day state capital was just a small settlement of a few peasants and some Benedictine monks from Lake Tegern. The site was known quite simply as "ze den Munichen", a dialect form of "zu den Mönchen" (the monks' place). Accordingly, the Munich coat of arms today bears the image of a child in a monk's habit, the "Münchner Kindl".

The settlement of the River Isar first attracted attention in 1156, when Heinrich der Löwe (Henry the Lion), Duke of Saxony and Bavaria and cousin of the German Emperor Frederick Barbarossa, was looking for a place to set up a toll station for the passage of salt, a lucrative product from nearby Salzburg. Until then, tolls had been collected by the powerful bishop of Freising at Oberföhring Bridge, a short distance to the north. Duke Heinrich burned the bridge down and established a new one, together with a market, customs house and mint, at a fork in the Isar.

Bishop Otto of Freising, himself an uncle of Frederick Barbarossa, protested to the emperor, who decided to leave Munich in his cousin Heinrich's hands, while granting one-third of the toll revenues to the diocese of Freising, dues that were paid until 1852. The day of the emperor's decision, June 14, 1158, is recognized as the date of Munich's founding.

The salt trade made Munich prosperous and the settlement grew rapidly into a proper town. In 1180, after Heinrich refused military aid for the emperor's foreign wars, Frederick Barbarossa threatened to raze Munich to the ground. But Uncle Otto pleaded the city's case, for the bishop of Freising was making more money from his share of the salt duty than he ever earned from the Oberföhring monopoly. The city was saved but taken away from Heinrich and handed over to the Wittelsbach family, who ruled Bavaria for the next seven centuries.

The city made a fortune from salt tolls collected by the River Isar.

The Wittelsbachs Take Over

By the end of the 13th century, Munich was the largest town in the Wittelsbach dominions. But the prosperous Munich burghers grew discontented and began to press Duke Ludwig the Stern (1229–94) for a larger piece of the pie. In defence, the duke built himself a fortress, the Alter Hof, parts of which can still be seen just west of the Hofbräuhaus.

Munich entered the international political arena when Duke Ludwig IV (1294–1347) was made Holy Roman Emperor in 1328. With his court firmly established in Munich, he enlisted scholars from all over Europe as his advisors in a form of royal academy. Most notable among them were Marsiglio of Padua and William of Occam, philosophers who defended secular power against that of the Pope and thus made themselves useful allies for Ludwig. William told him: "You defend me with your sword and I'll defend you with my pen." The philosopher became famous for a piece of common sense known as "Occam's Razor", which states, roughly, that if you've found a simple explanation for a problem, don't look for a complicated one. Bavarians like that kind of thinking.

Troubled Times

The Black Death brought devastation to Munich in 1348. The city suffered social unrest, abrupt economic decline and the debasement of its currency. In a mass psychotic reaction to the catastrophe, citizens went on a rampage, massacring Jews for alleged ritual murder.

High taxes and general penury resulted in a revolt of burghers against the patricians. In 1385, the people took cloth merchant Hans Impler from his house to the Schrannenplatz (now Marienplatz) and beheaded him. The patricians and their princes demanded draconian financial compensation and the situation deteriorated into open rebellion from 1397 to 1403.

By bringing in heavy military reinforcements, the Wittelsbachs regained the upper hand without making any of the far-reaching civic concessions won by the guilds of other German towns, such as Augsburg, Hamburg and Cologne. To secure their position in these troubled times, the Wittelsbachs built a sturdy Residenz on what was then the north-west corner of town. The massive, fortress-like palace (see p. 43) attests to the kind of protection the despotic monarchy needed.

Reform and Counter-Reform

Dissent eased in the 15th century and trade boomed in salt, wine and cloth. The town also served as a transit point for the rich "Venice goods" of spices and gold. Renewed prosperity made it possible to build the great Frauenkirche, still a town symbol, and the Gothic

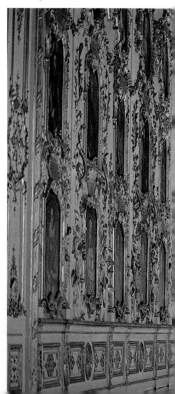

14

civic citadel of the Altes Rathaus.

By the middle of the 16th century, an architectural rivalry grew up between the burghers, who favoured the German Gothic style for their homes, and the Bavarian nobles, who preferred the Renaissance styles of Spain and Italy. The look of Munich in the 1500s is preserved in Jakob Sandtner's city model on display in the Bavarian National Museum (see p. 68). But the original construction was al-

The Wittelsbachs' Residenz was a huge fortress and opulent palace.

most completely replaced by the Baroque and Rococo palaces of the 17th and 18th centuries and the neo-Gothic and neo-Classical buildings of the Industrial Revolution.

The predilection of the Bavarian aristocracy for foreign artists was in many ways a reaction to the subversive implications of German nationalism which had grown out of the Reformation. In 1510, when Martin Luther passed through Munich on his way to Rome, his still relatively orthodox preaching met with sympathy. But, some ten years later, Luther's revolutionary positions aroused the ire of the traditionally conservative Bavarians, and Duke Wilhelm IV put into practice the severe measures advocated by the Jesuits. Rebellious monks and priests were arrested and executed; in 1527, the repression culminated in the drowning or burning of 29 members of Munich's Baptist community who refused to recant.

The religious conflict concealed a competition for political and economic power. The city's bourgeoisie had seen in the Reformation an opportunity to push for social reforms which the aristocracy had adamantly resisted. In the struggles that followed, the burghers were forced to relinquish the salt monopoly to the administration of the state.

With a certain vindictiveness, the nobles flaunted their political triumph with sumptuous festivities at court, such as those to pay homage to Emperor Charles V and his Spanish retinue during their Munich visit of 1530. The climax of pomp and circumstance in grand Renaissance style was achieved with the three-week-long wedding celebrations of Duke Wilhelm V and his bride, Renata of Lorraine, in 1568.

The patricians received spiritual support from the Jesuits, brought to Munich by Duke Wilhelm V to establish a school and to set up a theatre for the performance of morality plays. Some people resented this foreign influence, laying the foundation for the now perennial Bavarian distrust of outsiders.

Good Money After Bad
The extravagant expenditures of the aristocracy left the state coffers empty by the time Maximilian I (1573–1651) came to the throne. Although the Bavarian state was facing bankruptcy, Maximilian (who became Prince Elector in 1623) proceeded to build a magnificent collection of art works.

However painful this may have been for his tax-crippled subjects, we can be thankful to Maximilian for having thus laid the foundations of the Alte Pinakothek.

It was also Maximilian who ordered the splendid decorations that embellish the Residenz. Gustavus Adolphus of Sweden was so impressed with it when he invaded Munich in 1632, during the cruel Thirty Years' War, that he said he would have liked to carry the whole thing back to Stockholm on wheels. Instead, he settled for 42 Munich citizens, who were taken hostage against payment by Bavaria of 300,000 *Thaler* in war reparations. (All but six of them returned three years later.)

In the Thirty Years' War (1618–48), Munich suffered less damage by bombardment than many other German towns. But starvation and disease wrought more havoc than cannon, taking a toll of 7,000 inhabitants, one-third of the city's population. In 1638, Maximilian set up the Mariensäule (Column of the Virgin Mary) to commemorate the town's emergence from suffering.

The Prince Electors frequently involved their people in costly foreign adventures, rubbing salt into the wounds of Munich's civic poverty. In 1683, Max* II Emanuel decided to help the Austrians beat off the Turks besieging Vienna. He promptly set out for Belgrade and brought back 296 Turks as sedan-chair bearers and road-builders—Munich's first *Gastarbeiter* (immigrant workers). The Turkish Wars are commemorated in huge paintings that can be seen in Schleissheim Castle. The city's war debt was 20 million guilders.

In the War of the Spanish Succession (1701–14) Max Emanuel fought on the losing side, with the French, and Munich had to bear the burden of Austrian occupation from 1704 to 1714. When the farmers rebelled, the ringleaders were arrested and hung, drawn and quartered on Marienplatz. Their heads were displayed on pikes at Isar Gate.

After the war, the Bavarian aristocracy did not show itself sympathetic to the tribulations of the citizenry. The nobles set about building splendid little palaces, such as the Preysing, Erzbischöfliches (Archbishop's) and Törring-Jetten-

---

* "Max" is an accepted and not disrespectful Bavarian alternative to "Maximilian".

bach Palais (now the General Post Office), strategically situated near the Prince Elector's Residenz.

Peace in an English Garden

The people of Munich grew ever more xenophobic as Hungarian hussars took over the city in 1742. They were dispatched by Empress Maria Theresa in retaliation for the Bavarian Prince Elector's opposition to Austro-Hungarian involvement in Germany.

In this atmosphere of hostility, Maximilian III Joseph (1727–77) should not have been surprised when the Munich bourgeoisie resisted his attempt to establish a court monopoly on manufacturing. With the exception of Nymphenburg porcelain, which still thrives today, all the royal manufacturers went bankrupt. A brighter note was struck with the building of the delightful Cuvilliéstheater and the performance there by one Wolfgang Amadeus Mozart of his operas *The Abduction from the Seraglio, The Marriage of Figaro* and *The Magic Flute*.

In 1777, the Wittelsbach

Turkish workers—the backbone of Munich's municipal services.

succession fell to Karl Theodor, a member of the Mannheim branch of the family. He didn't want to leave Mannheim, he didn't like Munich and the feeling was mutual. The people were starving. There was no bread, but instead of wheat, Karl Theodor sent in soldiers to hold down the angry populace in those revolutionary times.

Benjamin Thompson, an American with British sympathies who had fled Rumford (later Concord), New Hampshire, during his own country's revolution, suggested a solution to Karl Theodor's predicament. With the prince's blessing, Count Rumford—as he was subsequently known—provided schools and work to keep the unruly soldiers off the streets. He set up workshops and soup kitchens for the poor. (The potato-and-barley soup that was dispensed there is served in Munich to this day as *Rumfordsuppe.*)

Then, in 1789, Rumford requisitioned a marshy wilderness on the outskirts of town and detailed the soldiers to drain it for development as a gigantic public park. The result of Rumford's efforts, the Englischer Garten, is a lasting monument to American enterprise and know-how. **19**

New Hopes, Ancient Dreams
While Munich was cultivating its garden, the rest of Europe was in a revolutionary uproar. But the city didn't remain isolated for long. In 1800, it was occupied by the French troops of General Jean Victor Moreau, who set up headquarters in Nymphenburg Palace.

Napoleon himself came to town in 1805 to celebrate the marriage of his wife Josephine's son, Eugène de Beauharnais, to Princess Augusta of Bavaria. The journey to Munich did not inconvenience the emperor too much, as it was on the way to Austerlitz, where he was to fight the Russians and Austrians. Napoleon elevated Max IV Joseph from Prince Elector to King of Bavaria and in exchange took a vast contingent of Bavarians on his Russian campaign of 1812, leaving 30,000 of them to die on the battlefield. Under pressure from the French, Max Joseph emancipated the Protestants of Munich, improved conditions for the Jews and introduced a more moderate Bavarian constitution.

And somehow, amid all the troubles of war and revolution, Munich managed to celebrate once again. Heeding the new spirit of the times, the royal court was wise enough not to exclude the populace from the wedding festivities of Max Joseph's son, Ludwig, to Theresa of Saxony. On October 17, 1810, horse races were organized with great success. They grew into an annual event, the world-famous Oktoberfest.

Munich itself was gradually

expanded to the north and west—into an area named Maxvorstadt—linking the centre to Schwabing. The Graeco-Roman architecture of the Nationaltheater brought to the city the first signs of the classical spirit that was to become the obsession of Ludwig I.

Born in Strasbourg, Ludwig (1786–1868) was determined to break the French stranglehold on German culture and make Munich a spearhead for a new nationalist movement. During the Napoleonic occupation, the civic symbol of the Münchner Kindl had been replaced with an imperial lion. Ludwig brought back the little monk.

Familiar with the architecture of Rome and the Greek monuments of Sicily, he wanted to turn Munich into an "Athens-on-the-Isar". He be-

Sober neo-Classicism replaced the exuberance of the 18th century.

gan by moving Bavaria's university from Landshut to Munich. It was established along Ludwigstrasse in the Schwabing area first developed under his father's rule.

He built majestic Odeonsplatz, with its Siegestor (Gate of Victory). However, the gate was scarred by bombs during World War II and since then it has become a symbol of defeat. But Königsplatz, with its Greek Revival architecture, was the most complete realization of Ludwig's classical aspirations. Typically, Ludwig laid the foundation stone for the Alte Pinakothek (the gallery designed to house the royal art collections) on April 7, 1826, the anniversary of the painter Raphael's birth.

A prodigious worker, rising before dawn each day to go to his office in the Residenz, the king felt himself entitled to some diversion from his sober duties and commissioned the painting of a series of portraits of the most beautiful young women of Munich. The collection hangs in the Schönheitengalerie (Gallery of Beautiful Women) at Nymphenburg Palace. Included is the likeness of his mistress, a dancer known as Lola Móntez, with whom he fell head over heels in love when he was 60 and

she 28. She was Ludwig's ruin. He made her the Countess von Landsfeld, to the horror both of his conservative ministers and the radical university students. In 1848, as revolution was sweeping Europe, the students and angry citizens of Munich forced Ludwig to deport Lola, and he himself abdicated in disgust.

Ludwig's successor, Maximilian II (1811-64), boosted Munich's cultural reputation thanks to his intimacy with illustrious thinkers such as historian Leopold von Ranke, philosopher Friedrich von Schelling and the chemist Justus von Liebig.

End of a Dream
The last great king of Bavaria was the romantic Ludwig II (1845-86), famous for his close relationship with Richard Wagner. Under Ludwig's patronage, the composer staged in Munich the premières of his operas *Tristan and Isolde, The Mastersingers of Nuremberg, Rhinegold,* and *Valkyrie.*

In the mundane world of 19th-century industrial expansion, Ludwig II dreamt of making Munich the music capital of the world. He wanted to build a gigantic theatre for his idol Wagner, a place where the composer could develop his concept of *Gesamtkunst-werk*—a synthesis of music, lyrics and theatre. But the banalities of state finances interfered and Bavarian politicians forced him to relinquish the project to Bayreuth.

Ludwig II adored French châteaux. At Linderhof he realized a dream.

Ludwig acted out his fantasies in the eccentric fairy-tale palaces he built outside Munich—a medieval castle at Neuschwanstein, a French château at Linderhof, and a fanciful version of Versailles' Grand Trianon at Herren-chiemsee. But it was at one castle that he didn't build, the

16th-century Schloss Berg on Lake Starnberg, that his life came to a sad and mysterious end.

Trompe-l'œil wall-painting recaptures Munich's war-bombed past.

By 1886, Ludwig's wild behaviour had persuaded the Bavarian government that he·was mad, and a special commission declared him as such. The director of a mental asylum accompanied him to Schloss Berg and the two were later found drowned. It was never determined whether murder or suicide was involved.

Uncle Luitpold took over as regent (ruling in place of Ludwig's brother, the insane King Otto). He presided over the grand *fin de siècle* artistic movement of the Jugendstil. This was followed a generation later by the Blaue Reiter school of Kandinsky, Klee and Marc. Writers such as Thomas Mann, Rilke and Stefan George moved to Schwabing. The artistic ferment also attracted a young painter from Vienna, an embittered fellow named Adolf Hitler.

The Wittelsbach dynasty, like the Habsburg in Vienna and the Hohenzollern in Berlin, ended in the disaster of World War I. Bavarians resented having been dragged into the European conflagration by what they felt was Prussian belligerence, and a new social democratic movement gained support. In November 1918, with the war in its last days, Kurt Eisner, a well-meaning but rather vague intellectual, led a march of workers and peasants from the Theresienwiese. En route, disaffected soldiers took control of their barracks and hoisted the red flag of revolution.

In the Mathäser Bräuhaus—breweries being a favoured spot for political action in Munich—the Bavarian Republic was declared. The people invaded the Residenz and wandered around hooting for echoes in the vast galleries and ballrooms. Ludwig III, the last Wittelsbach king, fled in a car from the palace.

But the new republic of workers, peasants and soldiers, modelled on the soviets of the Russian revolution, came under violent attack from the conservative press and private armies of troops *(Freikorps)* roaming the streets. Playing on Bavarian xenophobia, the right wing attacked Eisner as a Berliner and as a Jew. Just three months after the November revolution, Eisner was shot dead by a young aristocrat hoping to curry favour with an extreme right-wing club.

A group of "coffee-house anarchists" led by writers Ernst Toller and Erich Mühsam took over briefly, but they were quickly replaced by hardline communists. The Bavarian Red Army was then routed in bloody fighting with the Freikorps, and Bavaria as an independent republic was crushed.

In the space of six months, Munich had known in breathtaking succession a monarchy, revolutionary socialism, moderate socialism, anarchy, communism and brutal counter-revolutionary oppression. A tolerant tradition was swept away and the city became a breeding ground for extremist political and paramilitary groups.

Hitler's Munich
Adolf Hitler had first been drawn to Munich by its cultural ambience, but he remained immune to the innovative tendencies of the avant-garde. His own painting was stolidly academic and attracted no attention. He turned to the clamour of German nationalism and a chance photograph of a rally on Odeonsplatz in August 1914 shows Hitler in the crowd, joyfully greeting the declaration of war. **25**

He returned to Munich as a corporal in 1918. It was while working to re-educate soldiers in nationalistic, anti-Marxist ideas at the end of the Bavarian republic that he joined the Deutsche Arbeiter-Partei. By February 1920, he was addressing 2,000 members in the Hofbräuhaus. The association became known as the Nationalsozialistische Deutsche Arbeiter-Partei, or Nazi Party. Its symbol was the swastika. Armed storm troops of the party's Sturm-Abteilung (S.A.) went round Munich breaking up opposition political meetings.

At a January 1923 gathering, Hitler said: "Either the Nazi Party is the German movement of the future, in which case no devil can stop it, or it isn't, in which case it deserves to be destroyed." Both predictions proved true. By November, the party had 55,000 members and 15,000 storm troops—and Hitler felt strong enough to stage his famous Beer Hall Putsch.

It was intended as a first move in the campaign to force the Bavarian state government to cooperate in a Nazi march on Berlin. The putsch ended in a debacle on Odeonsplatz and Hitler was sent to prison, but not before he had turned the whole affair to his advantage.

Hitler made his trial for treason into an indictment of his prosecutors as accomplices of the "November criminals", who, he said, had stabbed Germany in the back in 1918 with their anti-war movement. He became an instant hero.

Beer, Bluff and Bullets

The Beer Hall Putsch, which launched Hitler's national career, was staged in the Bürgerbräukeller. It gave a foretaste of the crazy melodrama, bluff and shameless gall he was later to exhibit on the world scene.

With the Bavarian minister Gustav von Kahr about to speak, Hitler burst into the crowded room, smashed a beer mug to the floor and pushed forward at the head of his storm troops, brandishing a pistol. In the pandemonium, he jumped on a table and fired a shot into the ceiling to get the assembly's undivided attention. "National revolution has broken out!", he yelled. "Farce! South America!" replied a few wags, who were promptly beaten up. The new Hitler style of politics had arrived.

Today the Bürgerbräukeller has been replaced by the Hilton City Hotel. History pilgrims will find no plaque there commemorating the putsch.

In prison at nearby Landsberg, Hitler was treated as an honoured guest. He was not required to perform prison work, but held political meetings and wrote *Mein Kampf* instead.

Although Hitler's career took him to Berlin, the Nazis kept their party headquarters in Munich at the Brown House (the colour of their shirts). Brighter spirits such as whimsical comedian Karl Valentin and his great fan, dramatist Bertolt Brecht, also made their home in Munich, but the brown shirts triumphed.

In 1935, Munich was named "Capital of the (Nazi) Movement". It earned its status as the vanguard in June 1938, when the central synagogue was looted, five months before the *Kristallnacht* (Crystal Night) rampage that destroyed most of Germany's Jewish shops and houses of prayer.

In September of that year, Munich also became a symbol of the ignominious appeasement of Britain and France. Prime ministers Neville Chamberlain and Edouard Daladier came to the Bavarian capital to negotiate Czechoslovakia's dismemberment with Hitler and Mussolini. The meeting took place in the Führerbau. Later, Chamberlain asked the Führer to sign the piece of paper that the British leader was to wave at his people as a guarantee of "peace in our time".

War and Peace

A spark of resistance in wartime Munich came when two students, Hans and Sophie Scholl, courageously distributed anti-Hitler "White Rose" leaflets. But brother and sister were betrayed and executed.

World War II brought 71 air raids to the city, killing 6,000 and wounding 16,000. Bombardments, most intense in 1944, heavily damaged the Frauenkirche, St. Peter's and St. Michael's churches and large sections of the Residenz and Alte Pinakothek. The Brown House was destroyed but, ironically, most of Hitler's other buildings were left intact.

The post-war reconstruction was a triumph of hard work and fiercely loyal attachment to the great traditions of Munich's past. Monuments, palaces and churches have been restored with meticulous care. Traditionally open to the arts and good living in general, Munich rapidly expanded to become West Germany's third-largest city (population 1,263,000), welcoming many Berliners and refugees from the former eastern territories. **27**

Emphasizing its reputation for cheerfulness, the "Metropolis with a Heart" played proud host to the 1972 Olympic Games in an atmosphere that began in delightful serenity. But once again, the city came under a shadow as militant Palestinians raided the Olympic Village and killed 12 Israeli athletes.

There is clearly no formula for achieving immunity from world conflicts, but somehow Munich continues to express good will, German-style… sorry, Bavarian-style.

Finding Your Way…

Here are some common terms you may come across in Bavaria:

Allee	boulevard
Bahnhof	railway station
Brücke	bridge
Brunnen	fountain
Burg	castle, fortress
Dom	cathedral
Gasse	alley
Kirche	church
Markt	market
Rathaus	town hall
Platz	square
*Schloß**	castle, palace
See	lake
Stift	monastery
Straße	street
Ufer	river bank
Weg	path, way

* read ß as ss.

What to See

Munich has two enormous assets for the visitor. A large majority of museums, monuments, palaces and churches are concentrated in the Innenstadt (inner city), which makes it a great town for walking. And the superb public transport

system of buses, trams, underground *(U-Bahn)* and surface trains *(S-Bahn)*, brings all the other sights within easy reach.

Rather than tackle the complicated business of driving your car around town, find a parking place—almost impossible in the centre—and save the car for excursions. If you walk wherever you can, you'll see more of the town's bustling street life and drop in more easily on the outdoor cafés. You'll be able to indulge in the

Whichever way up you look at it, the Old Town Hall on Marienplatz makes a very colourful backdrop.

serendipity of discovering Munich's unexpected courtyard vistas and hidden alleyways. And you'll happen upon little bars and shops tucked away in odd corners that you would completely miss in a car.

So, apart from the section devoted to excursions, we offer you Munich as a series of walks.

Innenstadt

Munich long ago expanded beyond its confined medieval boundaries, and the old city wall has disappeared. However, the remains of three gates survive to indicate the perimeter of the inner city—Isartor, Karlstor and Sendlinger Tor—together with Odeonsplatz, a rendezvous for salt traders setting off in the 14th century for northern Germany. And, since Munich's earliest beginnings, Marienplatz has been at the heart of it all.

Marienplatz to Theatinerstrasse

Until the middle of the 19th century, the wheat market was held on **Marienplatz.** The square was the obvious site for the town hall and the place where criminals and other unpopular people were hanged.

Marienplatz was also the focus for the most extravagant wedding Munich has ever seen—that of Duke Wilhelm V to Renata of Lorraine in 1568. Almost inevitably, the square was chosen in 1972 as the central junction for the new U-Bahn and S-Bahn system.

Graced with tubs of flowers and outdoor cafés, Marienplatz today forms part of an attractive pedestrian zone. Here you'll see the **Mariensäule** (Column of the Virgin Mary), erected in 1638 by Maximilian I in gratitude for the town's deliverance from the Swedes during the Thirty Years' War. At the base of the column are a basilisk, dragon, serpent and lion—symbols of plague, hunger, heresy and war—each being vanquished by heroic child-angels. From the top of the monument, the majestic figure of Mary watches over Munich. Holding Jesus in her left arm and a sceptre in her right, she reminds citizens in a secular age of Munich's firmly religious foundation.

The square also sports the partially reconstructed 19th-century Fischbrunnen monument. Young butchers used to leap into the bronze fountain after completing their apprenticeship, but nowadays the tradition is kept up only by an occasional Fasching (carnival) reveller or happy soccer fan.

At the eastern end of Marienplatz stands the almost too picturesque **Altes Rathaus** (Old Town Hall), a gay example of Munich's efforts to reconstruct, rather than replace, the vestiges of its venerable past. This Gothic-style edifice, with a dove-grey façade, amber-tiled steeple and graceful little spires, captures the spirit of the 15th-century

original designed by Jörg von Halsbach (also called Jörg Ganghofer), though it isn't an exact replica. In any case, with the addition over the centuries of a Baroque onion-shaped cupola and then a too-conscientious "regothification", the building destroyed by Al-

There are sweeter rewards to sightseeing than cultural enrichment.

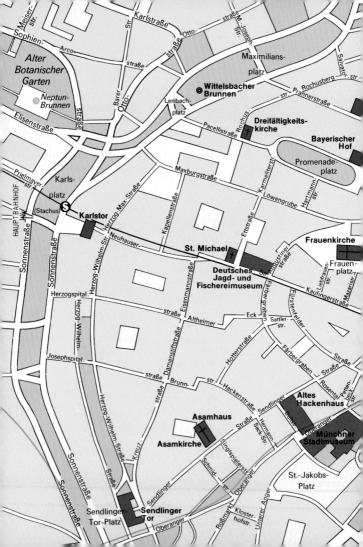

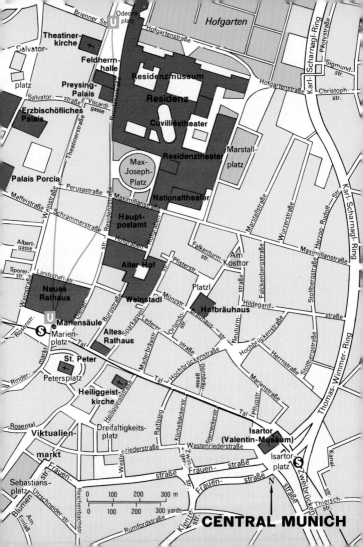

lied bombs was probably further from the original than what you see today. Apart from a banqueting hall on an upper floor, the Altes Rathaus fulfils a mainly decorative function.

The real business of city government takes place at the **Neues Rathaus** (New Town Hall) on the northern side of Marienplatz. This is a classic piece of 19th-century neo-Gothic—proud, self-assertive, its façade elaborately decorated with statues of kings, princes and dukes, saints, allegorical figures and characters from Munich folklore. The tower is around 260 feet high. Its main attraction—apart from the splendid view, if you want to take the lift to the top—is the 43-bell **Glockenspiel** (carillon) which goes wild every day at 11 a.m. (and at 5 p.m. in the summer). Two groups of figures appear, one re-enacting the tournament held during the wedding of Duke Wilhelm V and Renata of Lorraine and the other, underneath-re-creating the cooper's dance (*Schäfflertanz*) that was performed to exorcize the plague of 1517. Gone, however, are the nightwatchman blowing his horn, and the angel of peace blessing the little Munich monk (*Münchner Kindl*).

Now go up Weinstrasse (around the corner at the west end of the Neues Rathaus) and left along Sporerstrasse to the **Frauenkirche**, its full title being Domkirche zu Unserer Lieben Frau (Cathedral Church of Our Lady). This building, with its gold-tipped, bulbous domes atop mighty twin brick towers, dominates the Munich skyline and acts as a landmark and symbol for the city, just as the Empire State Building does for New York, or Big Ben for London. The church, an austere, unadorned Gothic structure, was built between 1468 and 1488 by Jörg von Halsbach. The Italian Renaissance domes are an addition of 1524.

The church is now undergoing extensive renovation and is not due to reopen until the middle of 1994.

Just outside the church, the granite fountain in Frauenplatz strikes a modern note. A waterfall plays and blocks of the stone have been arranged in the shape of an amphitheatre to provide seating. It's not a good idea, however, to stop here for a picnic.

West of the square, Augustinerstrasse leads to Neuhauser Strasse and what was once the church of the Augustinians. The building was

Worrisome Wind

Strange things can happen in Bavaria when the *Föhn* blows, most often in springtime. As a messenger from the Mediterranean on the other side of the Alps, this warm dry wind gusts down the mountains' northern slopes. It so clears the air that people in Munich get the optical illusion that the Alps have moved right up to the southern suburbs. If it gives some people migraine, others, often artists, claim phenomenally clear creative insights reminiscent of drug-induced conditions. Criminologists have also observed an increase of violence between husband and wife when the Föhn blows.

transformed into a customs house under Napoleon and then a hunting and fishing museum, the Deutsches Jagd- und Fischereimuseum, in 1966. Proclaimed by a wild boar in bronze, the collection will fascinate inveterate hunters and anglers.

Further along pedestrian-zoned Neuhauser Strasse is 16th-century **St. Michael's**, an Italian Renaissance church with Baroque overtones, the first of its kind in Germany, largely designed by the Dutch architect Friedrich Sustris. St. Michael epitomizes the combative spirit of the Counter-Reformation, and it is fitting that the secular defenders of the faith—the Wittelsbach dukes and German emperors—are portrayed on the gabled façade. Above the entrance, third figure from the right, stands the church's patron, Duke Wilhelm V (with a scale model of St. Michael's Church in his hand). Il Gesù, in Rome, provided the inspiration for the Baroque interior of St. Michael's, which surpasses the former in its masterful lighting.

Karlstor, a city gate dating from the 14th century, links Neuhauser Strasse to busy Karlsplatz, popularly known as the **Stachus** after an innkeeper named Eustachius Föderl. The Stachus conceals a veritable city of underground shops, which extend from the exit of the S-Bahn station. Walk north to Lenbachplatz and the city's loveliest fountain, the neo-Baroque **Wittelsbacher Brunnen** built by Adolf von Hildebrand at the end of the 19th century.

Pacellistrasse, east of Lenbachplatz, takes you past the distinctive faceted Baroque façade of the **Dreifaltigkeitskirche** (Trinity Church). In 1704 a young Munich girl, Anna Maria Lindmayr, dreamt that the city would be in-

vaded and destroyed unless a new church were constructed. Sure enough, the next year, during the War of the Spanish Succession, Austrian soldiers arrived; but work on the Dreifaltigkeitskirche didn't begin until 1711. The town was not destroyed.

Promenadeplatz is noted for the elegance of Palais Montgelas. This neo-Classical building today forms part of the posh Bayerischer Hof hotel, where you might like to refresh yourself with an expensive drink at the bar.

Valentin's Day
Although little known outside Germany, Karl Valentin was regarded by connoisseurs like the dramatist Bert Brecht as a comic genius equal to Charlie Chaplin. While resident in Munich in the early twenties, Brecht went almost every night to watch Valentin's portrayal of the clownish working-class characters of peasant origin peculiar to the city.

Valentin started out in beer halls, but he quickly attracted the attention of Schwabing's artists and intellectuals, who loved his insane, surreal logic. One of his most celebrated sketches involved his efforts to house birds in an aquarium and fish in a bird-cage.

Otherwise, continue north along Kardinal-Faulhaber-Strasse past the Palais Portia, one of Munich's first Baroque palaces and now a bank, to the **Erzbischöfliches Palais** (Archbishop's Palace) at number 7, a triumph of Rococo harmony with especially fine stucco work. Originally known as Palais Holnstein, it's the only 18th-century palace built by François Cuvilliés (see p. 44) to have survived intact to the present day.

End your walk in the shopping arcades of Theatinerstrasse and stop at a *Konditorei*, a café specializing in pastries and coffee.

Isartorplatz to Platzl

The sturdy **Isartor** in its restored form is the only city gate which retains its original 14th-century dimensions. It was put up in the days when the Bavarian Duke Ludwig IV was Holy Roman Emperor, and a fresco of 1835 on the arch of the gate shows the emperor returning triumphantly from victory over the Habsburgs. The Isartor now serves as a rather overgrown traffic island, but one of the towers houses a roof-top café and the Valentin-

Enjoy the fine Renaissance façade of St. Michael's. And a big pretzel.

Museum, devoted to the great cabaret comic of 1920s Munich, Karl Valentin (see box, p. 36).

From Isartor, walk along Tal, a shopping street that runs to **Heiliggeistkirche** (Church of the Holy Spirit). This 14th-century Gothic structure was extensively altered to the Baroque tastes of the 1720s. The two styles come together most notably in the **Marienaltar**—a beautiful wooden sculpture of 1450, the *Hammerthaler Mut-* *tergottes* (Hammerthal Mother of God) from the Lake Tegernsee monastery, set in an opulent gilded Baroque framework. The reconstructed high altar preserves a fine pair of *Adoring Angels* by Johann Georg Greiff, dated 1730.

West of Heiliggeistkirche, with an entrance on Rindermarkt, is **St. Peter's.** This is the oldest church in Munich, dating from before the foundation of the city itself in 1158. The original structure gave way to

a building in the Romanesque style, succeeded in time by a Gothic church with a twin-steepled tower. All but the tower was destroyed in the great fire of 1327 and a new Gothic structure went up. This was remodelled along Renaissance lines in the 17th century, and a tower with a single steeple was created. Destroyed in the war, St. Peter's has been faithfully reconstructed, down to the asymmetrically placed clocks on the tower. (Follow the crowd to the top for a stunning view of the inner city.)

The crowning piece of the light, bright interior is the **high altar** glorifying Peter and the fathers of the Church. It was restored from the remains of the 18th-century original, inspired by Bernini's altar for St. Peter's in Rome. Egid Quirin Asam (see p. 46) designed the ensemble, which incorporates Erasmus Grasser's *St. Peter*. The gilded wood figures of the Church fathers count among the masterpieces of Egid Asam.

Leading to the altar are splendid Rococo choir stalls. You'll also see Jan Polack's five Late Gothic paintings which once adorned the altar. They show Peter healing the lame, enthroned, at sea, in prison and on the cross. Also from the Late Gothic period is the Schrenk-Altar, a highly prized early 15th-century sandstone relief of the Crucifixion and the Day of Judgment.

Now duck along little Burgstrasse past the Altes Rathaus.

Pious frescoes on private houses are an honoured art in Munich, as exemplified here in Burgstrasse. **39**

Stop at number 5 to admire the **Weinstadl,** one of Munich's few remaining Gothic houses, once the home of the town clerk and now a tavern. Built around 1550, it has a neatly restored, leafy courtyard and staircase tower.

A miracle of inner-city tranquillity pervades the **Alter Hof.** The peaceful, tree-shaded square offers an exquisite panorama of medieval buildings. The reconstructed Burgtor (City Gate) and quaint little Affenturm (Monkey Tower) —incorporated in the west wing—recapture the atmosphere of the Wittelsbachs' first Munich residence as it was in the 15th century. The splendid heraldic painting on the tower came to light in the 1960s.

The Hof was originally built around 1255 on what was then the north-east corner of town, in defence against foreign invaders, as well as the city's own unruly burghers. It was subsequently superseded by the more massive Residenz. The old buildings suffered more from 19th-century urban development than from 20th-century bombs, but the careful reconstruction of the surviving south and west wings gives an idea of their former grandeur.

Turn right on Pfisterstrasse to Platzl (Little Square), the site of a building of no great architectural distinction but nonetheless the most publicized monument in Munich, the **Hofbräuhaus,** a beer hall.

Duke Wilhelm V founded a brewery in the Alter Hof in 1589 to avoid paying the high prices for imported beer from Hanover—this having always been just as much an aristocratic as a plebeian drink in Bavaria. It replaced wine as the staple alcoholic beverage after the Bavarian vineyards were destroyed during the cruel winters of the 13th and 14th centuries, making way for the sturdier hop and barley crops.

The brewery was first set up in the royal bath house, moving to more spacious quarters on Platzl in 1644. The Hofbräuhaus itself was built in 1896, after the brewery had been transferred to the other side of the River Isar. It soon became the most prestigious of Munich's political beer-hall arenas. In fact, in November 1921 Hitler's storm troops first gained notoriety in what became known as the "Schlacht im Hofbräuhaus" (Battle of the Hofbräuhaus). Today, the huge beer hall, with its long tables and oom-pah-pah music, is a magnet for tourists, but locals rarely gather here.

Odeonsplatz
to Maximilianstrasse

Odeonsplatz joins the inner city to Schwabing and the university. It's the point at which Ludwig I opened up the crowded heart of town to the more airy "Vorstadt", Schwabing then being no more than a suburb.

This noticeably airy and "liberating" walk begins in the Italian Renaissance-style **Hofgarten** (Court Garden), restored and replanted with the chestnut trees, flower beds and fountains specified in the original 17th-century plan. In the centre stands a 12-sided temple to Diana, topped by a rather sexy bronze statue of Bavaria. The arcades, decorated with frescoes of historic scenes featuring the Wittelsbachs, house art galleries and cafés. There's also a fascinating little **Theatermuseum** on the northern side (Galeriestrasse 4), worthwhile for the display of famous set designs from Munich's rich theatrical past.

Turn and look south-west across the Hofgarten to capture the delightful vista that helps to give Munich its peculiarly Mediterranean flavour—the twin towers and dome of the splendid **Theatinerkirche**. This Italian Baroque church was built between 1663 and 1688. Two Italian architects were involved, Agostino Barelli and Enrico Zuccalli. The façade was completed later by Cuvilliés.

The joyous impact of its silhouette on the city scene derives in part from the fact that the church was built to celebrate the birth of a baby boy to Princess Henriette Adelaide. This feeling of jubilation animates the rich decoration—ornamental vines, acanthus leaves and rosettes in the most spirited Italian Baroque style —and the splendid grey-and-white stucco embellishments in the cupola. Notice, too, the triumphant pulpit, the high altar (a copy of one destroyed by bombs) and, to the left, the Kajetan altar. This last was dedicated to St. Kajetan, founder of the Theatine Order commemorated in the church's title.

Across the street, facing Odeonsplatz, is the **Feldherrnhalle** (Hall of the Generals), a 19th-century monument to Bavarian military leaders. The building boasts statues of the Belgian-born Count Johann Tilly, a hero in the Thirty Years' War, and Prince Karl-Philipp von Wrede, victorious over the French in 1814. Less gloriously, it was the rendezvous for Nazi storm troops **41**

in Hitler's abortive putsch of 1923 and a focus for commemorative marches thereafter. Reinforcing the Italian atmosphere of the area, though with less of a light touch, the building is modelled after the Late Gothic Loggia dei Lanzi in Florence.

Next door, in Residenzstrasse, stands **Preysing-Palais,** the most richly ornamented of Munich's private Rococo palaces. Begun in 1723 by Joseph Effner, only the Residenzstrasse façade survived World War II, but the restoration of other parts was masterful. Take a look inside at the imposing ceremonial staircase.

At the other end of Residenzstrasse lies another jewel of 18th-century architecture, the **Hauptpostamt** or Main Post Office, formerly the Palais Törring-Jettenbach. You'll never buy a postage stamp in a more beautiful setting. The northern façade was given a face-lift in the 19th century to fit in with the classical demands of the Residenz and Nationaltheater on Maximilianstrasse. But the original Baroque doorway can be seen inside.

The Hofgarten and Theatinerkirche show the city's "Italian" side.

The **Nationaltheater** was completely rebuilt in 1963 as a copy of the original 1818 Greek-temple design by Karl von Fischer. The reconstruction epitomizes Bavarian traditionalism when it comes to cultural monuments.

The spacious **Max-Joseph-Platz** is named after the king whose statue sits in the centre. The fourth Max-Joseph of the Wittelsbach dynasty and the first—thanks to Napoleon—to be king, preferred what he felt would be a more dignified standing pose. But he died before the statue was completed and his son Ludwig I accepted the seated version.

The statue was placed alongside the greatest monument of Max-Joseph's family, the Wittelsbach **Residenz.** In 1385 the citizenry revolted, driving the dukes to construct lodgings safer than the Alter Hof (see p. 40). Over five centuries later, in 1918, another group of rebellious citizens pounded on the Residenz doors in the revolution that resulted in the short-lived Bavarian republic. The Wittelsbachs had to move out again, this time for good.

The German principalities were legion, and many of them rather frivolous, but the Residenz, now a museum, shows just how powerful and im-

43

mensely wealthy the proud Bavarian principality grew to be. To view the exterior, enter from Residenzstrasse and walk through the seven courtyards to Cuvilliéstheater, within the Residenz but not included on museum tours*.

The exquisite **Cuvilliéstheater,** or Altes Residenztheater, is one of the most enchanting playhouses in the world. Like its architect François de Cuvilliés, a dwarf from the Spanish Netherlands, the theatre is tiny, seating only 450. But its festive intimacy makes every performance a cosy gala. The four-tiered, horseshoe-shaped auditorium basks in a gilded Rococo décor of Greek nymphs, gods and goddesses— Bacchus, Apollo, Diana— and, with delicious incongruity, an American Indian girl complete with feather headdress, bow, arrows and cactus. The acoustics are correspondingly warm and golden—totally appropriate to the Mozart works played here for the past 200 years.

Cuvilliéstheater was preserved to the present day by a stroke of foresight. In 1943, the stucco ornamentation and sculpture were dismantled bit by bit. Some 30,000 separate pieces were carried away and stored in the vaults of various castles around Munich. Six weeks later the theatre building was gutted by fire bombs. And fifteen years elapsed before the 30,000 pieces were brought out of hiding and put together again.

* For a description of Munich's museums, see pp. 61–72.

Sendlinger Tor to Viktualienmarkt

The walk from Sendlinger Tor takes you through a popular district of the city centre, the busy shopping area of Sendlinger Strasse, and on past the municipal museum to the open-air market beside St. Peter's church. Only two hexagonal towers remain from the picturesque 14th-century **Sendlinger Tor** (City Gate).

Facing north-east, take the left fork along Sendlinger

Cuvilliés Altes Residenztheater, an exquisite setting for Mozart.

Walking's a joy: from Sendlinger Tor fountains to Viktualienmarkt.

Strasse to **Asamhaus** (number 61) where Egid Quirin Asam, master sculptor and architect of the 18th century, had his home. He was assisted in the decoration of the building by his brother, Cosmas Damian, who specialized in fresco painting. The ornate forenames of the brothers—probably their fathers's revenge for his own mundane Hans Georg—are appropriate to the rich Baroque style favoured by the two.

Stand on the opposite side of Sendlinger Strasse and look at the marvellously intricate façade of the house, dated 1733. Secure in their Catholic faith, the Asams happily mixed pagan and Christian figures in their decorative schemes. Just below the roof to the right (directly above the doorway*) you'll see a representation in stucco of heaven and the monogram of Christ. Below that appears the seated figure of Mary. But to the left is vine-bedecked Olympus, and Apollo with the triumphant gods of Fame and Fortune. Pegasus,

---

* The original doorway, depicting scenes from the Old and New Testaments, is now displayed in the Bavarian National Museum (see p. 68).

the flying horse, leaps up to them, while, lower down, a riot of nymphs and satyrs dance around the Muses of painting, sculpture and architecture.

The decoration of Asamhaus is marked by enormous diligence and ingenuity. It also confirms the brothers' light-hearted devotion to the good life and the inspiration of their religion.

The ultimate demonstration of this can be seen next door in the Asams' private church of St. Johann Nepomuk, originally linked to Egid Quirin's house by a special entrance. Popularly known as **Asamkirche,** the church was completed

in 1746. It was built at Egid Quirin's own expense and so liberated from the constraints of a patron's demands. The result is a subjective celebration of faith and life.

The variegated marble façade serves as a street-altar for passers-by on busy Sendlinger Strasse. It incorporates unhewn rocks originally intended for a fountain, and a statue of John of Nepomuk, a Bohemian saint popular in 18th-century Bavaria, presides over the porch. Inside, the two-tiered **high altar** carries the eye upwards to a towering Crucifixion dominated by a representation of God the **47**

Father, wearing the papal crown. Around this formidable monument all is movement and light, aglow still with the Asams' enthusiasm despite the effects of wartime destruction.

The imposing four-storey **Altes Hackerhaus** stands on the corner of Hackenstrasse. This rare surviving example of a private dwelling in the classical style has a succession of nine Doric, Ionic and Corinthian pillars running along each façade. The courtyard is especially picturesque. Further along Hackenstrasse, at the corner of Hotterstrasse, you'll find Munich's oldest operating tavern, Gaststätte zur Hundskugel, serving beer since 1440.

Double back across Sendlinger Strasse to St.-Jakobs-Platz and the fascinating **Münchner Stadtmuseum** (Municipal Museum; see p. 69). To the east of the museum lies one of the most colourful places in Munich and a meeting place for anybody with a fine nose—the **Viktualienmarkt,** what Charles Dickens would have called a "vittles market". Since 1807 the city's central food market has stood here. Stroll around the enticing stalls with their myriad cheeses and exotic spices, breads and meats. The cornucopia of vegetables and fruit prove better than any-

thing else that Munich is a crossroads of northern and southern Europe, and a gateway to the East, too.

The cheerful atmosphere of the market makes it the perfect place for annual performances of the Marketwomen's Dance on Shrove Tuesday. It's also the scene of lively celebrations around the flower-bedecked maypole.

Around Königsplatz

Königsplatz represents a convergence of the noblest and basest aspirations in the last several hundred years of Munich's history. When he was still crown prince, Ludwig I visualized the square as a second Acropolis, a vast open space surrounded by classical temples. There was no particular reason for the choice of this site, no junction of roads, for example. But Ludwig overrode the customary demands of urban planning, and workmen were soon widening stately Brienner Strasse, the street which took the royal family from the Residenz to Nymphenburg Palace.

After inspecting the Greek art on Königsplatz, what do we do next?

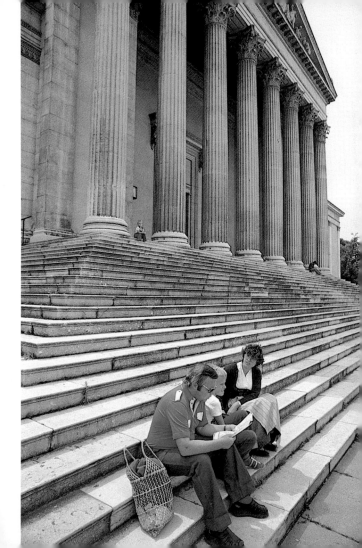

With Leo von Klenze as his architect, Ludwig made the square a grass-covered, tree-lined haven of tranquillity. A hundred years later, Hitler cut down the trees and paved over the grass for the troops and armoured cars of his military parades. (The pompous Nazi Ehrentempel, or Temple of Honour, which stood at the eastern end of the square, was deliberately blown up by Allied military engineers in 1945.) Today Königsplatz is returning to its original serenity, and the greenery is back.

The U-Bahn station brings you out beside the **Propyläen** (Propylaeum), modelled after the entranceway to the Acropolis in Athens. But this splendid monument to Ludwig's sublime imperviousness to functional considerations doesn't lead anywhere, for it closes off Königsplatz rather than providing access to the square. And despite the Doric columns, it's not even properly Greek, since the central "gateway" is flanked by two Egyptian-style pylons or towers. But the friezes that decorate them show the Wittelsbachs' special attachment to things Greek. They depict the Greek war of liberation from the Turks and the Greek people paying **50** homage to Ludwig's son Otto when he was made their king in 1832.

Before visiting the monuments on Königsplatz, continue past the Propyläen to **Lenbachhaus** on Luisenstrasse, an elegant ochre-coloured villa of the 1880s built in the style of Renaissance Florence and reconstructed after World War II. Like Egid Quirin Asam, the wealthy academic painter Franz von Lenbach, a darling of the German aristocracy, built himself a showy palace with the fortune accumulated from his art. Today the villa houses the excellent **Städtische Galerie*** of 19th- and 20th-century art. Coffee is served on the terrace or in the pleasant garden. In the little park opposite, you can play open-air chess on big stone boards.

The **Staatliche Antikensammlungen*** (Classical Art Collections), on the south side of Königsplatz, seems somewhat clumsy in design, with Corinthian columns set on an excessively elevated pedestal. Across the square stands the companion building, the **Glyptothek*** (Sculpture Museum). Designed in 1815 by von Klenze to house Ludwig I's collection of Greek and Roman sculpture, it was the first public museum building planned for that purpose.

Just across Gabelsberger Strasse, you come to another venerable art institution, the **Alte Pinakothek***. Ludwig commissioned von Klenze to provide a design for a monumental museum in the style of an Italian Renaissance palace. Reconstruction in 1958 preserved the spacious layout of galleries and cabinets on two floors, while imposing the excellent natural and artificial lighting characteristic of Munich museums.

North of nearby Theresienstrasse is the strikingly modern **Neue Pinakothek*** building, opened to the public in 1981. The work of Alexander von Branca, the elegant grey sandstone-and-granite structure replaces the old one destroyed in World War II. Extensive skylights provide superb natural lighting. The architecture breaks with the Alte Pinakothek's classical traditions, but achieves a nice harmony nonetheless.

In case you think it is too facile to relentlessly attack Hitler's legacy in Munich, take a look for yourself at two surviving examples of his architectural contribution to the city: the so-called Führer's Buildings *(Führerbauten)* at the east end of Königsplatz. It was at Arcisstrasse 12, now a music academy *(Musikhochschule)*, that Hitler received Chamberlain and Daladier, the British and French prime ministers who accepted the infamous Munich agreement of 1938 (see p. 27). Meiserstrasse 10 today houses important archaeological and art-historical institutions, but it was built in 1933 as an administrative centre for the Nazi Party. These grim, bunker-like blocks, designed by Paul Ludwig Troost under the obsessive supervision of Hitler himself, miraculously survived the American bombardments which devastated the Glyptothek and Staatliche Antikensammlungen.

Rather than finish the walk on this sombre note, continue down Meiserstrasse to the **Alter Botanischer Garten.** The town's major botanical garden is now situated at Nymphenburg Palace (see p. 77), but the lawns here still make for a pleasant stroll. Take a seat by the Neptune Fountain and look over the trees at the two cupolas of the Frauenkirche. And remind yourself that the people of Munich found time to lay out this lovely little spot in the middle of the Napoleonic Wars.

* See Museums section, pp. 61–72.

💼 Schwabing

The Schwabing district belongs to that select group of places around the world—London's Chelsea, Paris's Montparnasse, New York's Greenwich Village —of which it's said, often glibly but nonetheless accurately, that it is not so much a place as a state of mind.

Begin your walk symbolically—Munich loves its symbols —at the **Siegestor** (Victory Gate), which marks the southern boundary of Schwabing. This triumphal arch was designed for Ludwig I as a monument to the Bavarian army. In 1944 it was badly damaged, and in 1958 only partially restored, leaving the scars of war and a new inscription on the south side: *Dem Sieg geweiht, im Krieg zerstört, zum Frieden mahnend* (Dedicated to victory, destroyed in war, exhorting to peace). More than any other part of Munich, Schwabing epitomizes a break with military traditions.

Walk to the entrance of the University and you'll see the little square named Geschwister-Scholl-Platz after the brother and sister who gave their lives in the struggle against Hitler (see p. 27). Across the street stands St. Ludwig's, a neo-Romanesque

Free for All

During Schwabing's heyday at the turn of the 20th century, when artists, writers and their hangers-on flocked to Munich, townspeople revelled in the creative atmosphere of this bohemian area. Thomas Mann made his home here, as did Frank Wedekind and Bert Brecht, Wassily Kandinsky and Paul Klee. Other illustrious residents included Franz Marc, Rainer Maria Rilke and the symbolist poet Stefan George.

A countess-turned-bohemian, Franziska zu Reventlow, chronicled the neighbourhood's free love, free art, freedom for all and everything; she died penniless from the appropriately romantic illness of tuberculosis. Schwabing was the natural home of the biting satirical weekly *Simplicissimus* and the art magazine *Jugend*, which gave its name to the German version of Art Nouveau—Jugendstil.

A last moment of glory came in 1919 when the "Coffeehouse Anarchists", dramatist Ernst Toller and poet Erich Mühsam, took power after the assassination of prime minister Kurt Eisner. For all of six days—till the communists pushed the poets out—Schwabing ruled Bavaria, proclaiming the republic a "meadow full of flowers".

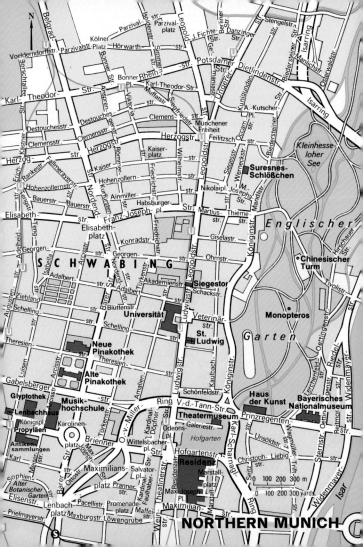

NORTHERN MUNICH

church distinguished mainly for the gigantic fresco of the *Last Judgment* in the choir by Peter Cornelius (1836). At least in terms of size, it's the world's second-greatest fresco (60 by 37 feet) after Michelangelo's in the Sistine Chapel.

At night the bohemian spirit of Schwabing animates wide and breezy **Leopoldstrasse,** the street that begins north of Siegestor. The great writers and artists of the past may have disappeared, but the art galleries and cafés are still going strong. Even though the intellectual ferment doesn't bubble as much as before, you sense an underlying excitement as you walk along what local wags call Boulevard Leopold. Having provided a focus for the avant-garde of Jugendstil and the Blaue Reiter, Schwabing now serves as the meeting place for the talents of the new German cinema. You may well catch a glimpse of the latest directors or actors in

vogue, or at least those aspiring to stardom.

At Münchener Freiheit, road junction and U-Bahn stop, cut down Feilitzschstrasse to **Wedekindplatz,** a centre of the theatre, cabaret and café life that in its best moments recaptures the golden past. Continue to nearby Werneckstrasse and **Suresnes-Schlösschen** (Little Château), now the Catholic Academy, designed in 1718 for Prince Elector Max Emanuel. It was built to remind him of the ten happy years he spent in exile west of Paris during the War of the Spanish Succession at the French château of the same name. The Baroque structure went through several neo-Classical remodellings in the 19th century, but some of the original stucco work can still be seen.

Schwabing street theatre draws on the talents of local students.

Olympiapark

Munich's Olympic centre contains some outstanding examples of contemporary architecture. The stadium, sports hall and swimming pools, built for the 1972 Olympic Games, are linked by a spectacular tent-like roof of transparent acrylic which, on a rainy day, resembles a giant spider's web.

The surrounding park, now used for summer theatre and arts festivals, has a man-made lake and artificial, grass-covered hillocks. There's a revolving restaurant and an observation deck half-way up the 950-foot-high Olympic Tower, used for telecommunications.

Just north-east, across the Petuel Ring Autobahn, you can see the curved aluminium skyscraper built as headquarters for the Bavarian Motor Works in 1972. It's known locally as the "four-cylinder". Alongside, in an upturned dome, is the fascinating BMW-Museum (see p. 72).

Englischer Garten Area

From Schwabing, head east to the **Englischer Garten.** Opened in 1793, the park was the brainchild of an American-born adventurer who had fought on the British side during the American Revolution. Benjamin Thompson, better known to Bavarians as Count von Rumford (see p. 19), drew on the ideas of the great Eng-lish landscape gardeners, Capability Brown and William Chambers. In fact, the Chinesischer Turm (Chinese Tower), the decorative pagoda that serves as a bandstand for a popular beer garden, was directly inspired by Chambers' Cantonese Pagoda in London's Kew Gardens.

Breaking with the French tradition of geometric avenues, elaborately sculptured trees and hedges favoured by the Bavarian aristocracy, Rumford and his German associate Ludwig von Sckell preferred a "natural" grouping of hills, dells and babbling brooks. In keeping with their revolutionary populist ideas, they wanted to create a garden for Munich's poor. Prince Karl Theodor had been under the impression that the Englischer Garten would be no more than an elaborate extension of the Hofgarten, until he saw pigs and cattle grazing where once his lords had hunted for pheasant and stags, and potato patches in place of exotic flowers.

Today the pigs and potatoes have gone, but the natural landscaping is still a joy for picnickers, lovers and all well-meaning loiterers. The Monopteros (love temple) atop a grassy mound south of the 57

A young musician earns her keep as others walk in Englischer Garten.

Chinese Tower attracts the more colourful residents of Schwabing. They bask in a haze of Oriental herbs, admiring the splendid view of the old city.

The gardens stretch 3 miles to the north, making a lovely walk along the swiftly flowing River Isar. Stroll up to the Kleinhesseloher See, a pond that offers some boating for the more energetic. The little Eisbach, a branch of the Isar, rushes helter-skelter under Tivoli Bridge like a veritable mountain rapid, encouraging a particularly breakneck version of wind-surfing. It's a great spectator sport, but if the mere sight of such activity exhausts you, head for the pretty Japanese Tea House (in the southwest corner), donated by Japan in honour of the 1972 Olympic Games.

Just beyond the Tea House, on the southern edge of the garden at Prinzregentenstrasse 1, stands the **Haus der Kunst** (House of Art), a venue for temporary exhibitions and home of the Staatsgalerie moderner Kunst (State Modern Art Gallery; see p. 72). The Haus der Kunst is another building of the Hitler era that Allied bombardments missed. In the bad old days it was known as the Haus der deutschen Kunst (House of German Art), a temple to Hitler's personal vision of a truly German art. The monotonous pile, once again by Paul Ludwig Troost, was quickly endowed with popular nicknames— "Münchner Kunstterminus" (Munich Art Terminal) and "Palazzo Kitschi".

Another museum lies further along Prinzregentenstrasse, the **Bayerisches Nationalmuseum** (Bavarian National Museum; see p. 68). From here, walk across Prinzregentenbrücke, **59**

Degenerates Forever!

Hitler's speech inaugurating the Haus der deutschen Kunst in 1937 attacked the "obscenities" of avant-garde art and specifically forbade any painter to use colours that the "normal" eye could not perceive in nature. Two exhibitions were staged to distinguish the good from the bad: one of so-called great German art, the other of officially designated degenerate art.

The trouble was that people preferred the "degenerate" stuff, which attracted a crowd of 2 million, five times as many as the other exhibition. Afterwards, many of these paintings were hidden away. Back in the Haus der Kunst today, they include works by Kandinsky, Mondrian, Kokoschka and Chagall.

spanning the River Isar to the winged **Friedensengel** (Peace Angel). High on her pillar, she surveys Prinzregententerrasse, a pleasant Florentine-style promenade surrounded by gardens. Begun in 1896, the monument celebrates the 25 years of peace that followed the German defeat of the French in 1871. Portraits of the architects of that peace—Bismarck, Kaisers Wilhelm I and II and Generals Moltke and von der Tann—decorate the monument. But the mosaics of *Peace, War, Victory* and the *Blessings of Culture* indicate the rather ambiguous nature of the celebration.

There's nothing ambiguous about the charming **Villa Stuck** (Prinzregentenstrasse 60), built in 1898 for the last of Munich's painter-princes, Franz von Stuck. He amassed a fortune rivalling that of Lenbach by astutely combining the new trends of Jugendstil symbolism with the prevailing salon style for a certain luxury spiced with a dash of decadence. The opulent villa makes the perfect setting for the Jugendstil Museum. All the interior decoration and furniture date from the turn of the century. The house, guarded by Stuck's bold equestrian *Amazone,* is a venue for temporary exhibitions.

To the south lies the phenomenal **Deutsches Museum** (see p. 66) of science and technology. And on the west bank of the Isar, opposite the museum, rises the controversial European Patent Office *(Europäisches Patentamt).* This black steel-and-glass structure has a cool elegance that many find admirable, while others regret the old neighbourhood that had to make way for it.

Museums

The number and diversity of museums and galleries in Munich attest to the city's importance as a cultural centre. For an indication of hours and closing days, see page 116.

Alte Pinakothek

This is one of the world's great art museums, in a class with the Louvre of Paris, the Uffizi of Florence, the Prado of Madrid and New York's Metropolitan.

The gallery (Barer Strasse 27) is the perfect expression of Bavaria's centuries-old dedication to the arts and, more particularly, the resolution of the Wittelsbachs to invest in the great glory of painting. That glory draws not only on the German masters, but also on the highest achievements of the Flemish, the Dutch, the Italians, Spanish and French.

The creation of what is now the Alte Pinakothek began in earnest in the 17th century when Maximilian I installed a Kammergalerie (art gallery) in the Residenz for pictures acquired by his great-grandfather Wilhelm IV, as well as his own growing collection of Dürers and superb German triptychs. Then Max Emanuel lost his head and bought 105 paintings by Rubens in 1689; it took 80 years to pay for them all. Ludwig I, who struggled for 20 years to acquire a Raphael *Madonna* and several other Italian masterworks, commented: "If the money were lost on gambling or horses, people would say that's the way it should be, but you spend it on art and they call it waste."

Here are the highlights of the collection:

One of the outstanding German works is the *Kirchenväteraltar* (Altar of the Church Fathers) painted around 1480 by **Michael Pacher.** This splendid polyptych of Saints Jerome, Augustine, Gregory and Ambrose was brought from the South Tyrol during the French Revolution.

On a less monumental scale are two exquisite little paintings of the 15th-century Cologne school by **Stefan Lochner,** *Maria im Rosenhag* (Mary in the Rose Garden) and *Anbetung des Christkindes* (Adoration of the Christ Child).

Pieter Brueghel the Elder produced *Das Schlaraffenland* (Fool's Paradise) in 1567. The artist only half-playfully shows a soldier, a peasant and a scholar sprawled on the ground—at a time when Brueghel wanted **61**

to arouse them to the evils of Spanish military occupation. The gawking *Kopf einer alten Bäuerin* (Head of an Old Peasant Woman) makes no concessions to flattery.

Roger van der Weyden's *Anbetung der Könige* (Adoration of the Magi), a devotional work of 1460, still evokes an attitude of reverence. However, in **Hans Memling's** *Die Sieben Freuden Mariens* (The Seven Joys of Mary), the religious theme is overwhelmed by the setting, a meticulously painted northern landscape.

Albrecht Dürer's *Vier Apostel* (Four Apostles), executed in 1526, is a noble portrayal of John with Peter, and Paul with Mark. The strips of text from Martin Luther's Bible were removed by Maximilian I because he was apparently afraid

Munich's Alte Pinakothek is one of the world's great museums; put aside enough time to visit it.

of criticism by the Jesuits. Another great Dürer is his *Self-portrait* of 1500, imbued with great vanity (note the Christ-like pose), but nonetheless masterful.

His contemporary, **Matthias Grünewald,** is much more down-to-earth, both in the gentle *Hl. Erasmus und Hl. Mauritius im Gespräch vertieft* (Conversation of St. Erasmus and St. Mauritius) and in the *Verspottung Christi* (Mocking of Christ) at once harsh and moving. The Wittelsbachs' first great acquisition was **Albrecht Altdorfer's** *Alexanderschlacht* (1529), Alexander's victory over Darius of Persia in 333 B.C. This fervent depiction of the western world's triumph over the Orient was a favourite of Napoleon's and hung in his apartments at St. Cloud.

Peter Paul Rubens is magnificently represented by a vast panoply of his talent. In *Das grosse Jüngste Gericht* (The Great Last Judgment), an enormous work of 1615, a terrible hustle among the damned and the saved takes place on an area of 6 yards by 4. The Jesuits removed the painting from their high altar at Neuburg because they found the nudity offensive. The loving portrait of Rubens' second wife, Hélène Fourment, in her wedding dress (1630) adopts a quieter note.

One of the more intriguing of **Anthony van Dyck's** portraits, *Die Gambenspielerin* (The Viola-da-gamba Player), captures the appeal of a girl who manages to look both haughty and charming.

Of all the self-portraits **Rembrandt** painted, one of the most interesting shows the artist as a young man of 23 in 1629, looking quite surprised, perhaps, by his own talent. The face appears again in *Die Kreuzabnahme* (The Removal of Christ from the Cross), 1633, in the young man next to the ladder. This painting is part of a cycle devoted to the Passion of Christ, another particularly gripping work being *Die Auferstehung* (The Resurrection).

Typical of **Frans Hals's** work is a revealing portrait of an arrogant merchant, *Willem van Heythuysen.*

A representative early work of **Leonardo da Vinci,** *Maria mit dem Kinde* (Mary with Child) was probably painted in 1473, when he was 21. It already possesses much of the serene power of his mature masterpieces.

Munich is also privileged to have one of **Titian's** superb **63**

Other Museums

Tourists too frequently neglect the excellent **Bayerisches Nationalmuseum** (Bavarian National Museum) in Prinzregentenstrasse), built in 1900. The exterior traces in different architectural styles the artistic evolution of the periods exhibited inside—a Romanesque east wing, Renaissance western façade, Baroque tower and Rococo west wing. The collection provides a truly magnificent survey of German cultural history from the Roman era, through the Middle Ages to the 19th century. It emphasizes both religious and secular arts and craftsmanship.

There are fine Romanesque and Gothic stone carvings, wooden sculptures and paintings from churches and abbeys long since disappeared or transformed. The outstanding pieces include *Inthronisierte Maria* (Enthroned Mary) from Perugia (1200), *Hl. Katerina* (St. Catherine) from Salzburg (1420) and a beautifully ornate polychrome wood *Maria im Rosenhag* (Mary in a Rose Bower) from Straubing (1320), showing Mary as the proudest of mothers and Jesus still a playful little boy.

The highlight for many proves to be the collection of wooden sculptures by Tilman Riemenschneider, Germany's great Late Gothic master, in the **Riemenschneider-Saal.** There are powerful statues of Mary Magdalene, St. Sebastian and the Apostles, carved around 1500.

Among other Late Gothic exhibits is one of the most frightening chiming clocks you're ever likely to come across, from the Heilbronn Monastery. The implications of *tempus fugit* were hammered home by a furious figure of Death riding a frantic-looking lion.

But notice, too, such admirable secular exhibits as the **Augsburger Weberstube,** a room decorated with the original medieval furnishings and carvings of the Augsburg Weavers' Guild. And the **Stadtmodell-Saal,** with Jakob Sandtner's intricate 16th-century scale models of Bavarian ducal cities, Munich taking pride of place beside Ingolstadt and Landshut. Lastly, look for the glorious carved doors illustrating Old and New Testament scenes, from Egid Quirin Asam's house on Sendlinger Strasse.

In the east wing of the museum, entered from Lerchenfeldstrasse, is the **Prähistorische Staatssammlung** (Prehistoric Museum), devoted to

Life-like marionettes create a dream-world all their own on the top floor of the Municipal Museum.

Bavarian finds from earliest Celtic times.

The **Münchner Stadtmuseum** (Municipal Museum) in St.-Jakobs-Platz reflects Munich's distinctive personality, and it's well worth spending an hour or two here to get a feel of the town's development since the Middle Ages. The Moriskenraum houses the museum's main attraction: merry wooden carvings of **Morris Dancers** from the Altes Rathaus council chamber. Dated 1480, they are magnificent examples of Erasmus Grasser's Gothic style.

Maps, models and photographs on the first floor illustrate Munich's rich history. On the second floor, 20 rooms have been furnished colourfully in various decorative styles from the past. You'll see kitchens, living rooms and bedrooms, examples of sumptuous rooms from the Residenz and cosy bourgeois homes of the 19th century complete with heavy Biedermeier pieces or the more delicate Jugendstil. Highlights include a very inviting 18th-century Weinstube (wine tavern) and a recon- **69** struction of an opulent artist's studio (Makart-Zimmer).

The fashion collection shows the evolution of styles in a town that has long been a centre of German design. A poignant effort has been made to inject a light touch into the display of wartime fashions.

Children (and adults, too) will love the **Puppentheater-Sammlung** (Marionette Theatre Collection) on the third floor, one of the largest of its kind in the world; Bavaria has long been a centre for the production of glove-puppets, shadow plays and mechanical toys.

On the other hand, the ground-floor **Deutsches Brauereimuseum** (German Brewery Museum) caters particularly to adults. This museum-within-a-museum explores the history of Germany's national drink, beginning with the year 3000 B.C. and the sculpture of an Egyptian brewery worker. The exhibition approvingly quotes the first literary allusion to the noble liquid in the *Epic of Gilgamesh*, the tale of a legendary Babylonian hero who apparently said: "Eat bread, you need it to live. Drink beer, it's the local custom." There's also a comprehensive selection of drinking vessels.

Scholars commissioned by King Ludwig I scouted the classical world for suitable works to display in the **Glyptothek** (Sculpture Museum) on Königsplatz. Some 160 pieces found a spacious home in the massive, Ionic-columned edifice, rebuilt after World War II. The Glyptothek glories in its great treasure, the **sculpture from the gables of the Temple of Aphaia,** found on the Greek island of Aegina. The well-preserved friezes date from 505 B.C. (west gable) and 485 B.C. (east gable). They show warriors with their shields fighting to defend the island's patron goddess, smiling that rather smug Ancient Greek smile. Look out, too, for other works of major importance: the *Apollo of Tenea*, a *Medusa*, the goddess of peace *Irene* and the *Barberini Faun* (named after a 17th-century Italian family of classicists).

The valuable displays of the **Antikensammlungen** (Classical Art Collections) include a lovely series of Greek vases and urns and, above all, the highly prized collection of Etruscan gold and silver formed by James Loeb. This German-American benefactor is well known to schoolchildren for the famous Loeb's Classical Library of Greek and Latin texts.

The 22-room **Neue Pinako-thek** in Barer Strasse emphasizes 19th-century German art, placed in a historical context of English 18th- and 19th-century portraits and landscapes and 19th-century French naturalist and Impressionist works.

A harsh still-life by Goya, *Gerupfte Pute* (Plucked Turkey), hangs here, together with a piercing study of the artist's doctor, *Don José Queralto*. This portrait is believed to be particularly complimentary because the subject had

This Improvisation *by Kandinsky is on display at Lenbachhaus.*

cured Goya of a recurring disease.

Look, too, for Turner's superb *Ostende*, Manet's *Frühstück* (Breakfast) and Van Gogh's *Vase mit Sonnenblumen* (Vase with Sunflowers). There are also many fine German works: *Riesengebirgslandschaft mit aufsteigendem Nebel* (Sudeten Mountains with Rising Mist) by Caspar David Friedrich delicately expresses the Romantic spirit. You'll be charmed by the wit of Karl Spitzweg, especially his *Armer Poet* (Poor Poet), a caricature of the romantic view of artistic squalor. And to round off your survey, there's the social realism of Max Liebermann and the Jugendstil symbolism of Gustav Klimt, Max Klinger and Franz von Stuck.

The **BMW-Museum,** off the Petuel Ring Autobahn, provides a fascinating look at the history of the Bavarian Motor Works. You'll see the cars motorcycles and aircraft engines that made BMW famous: all the classic originals are on display. But officials also had the excellent idea of relating a parallel history of the world events that occurred while these technical innovations were being made.

Against a stark background that makes artful use of lighting to highlight the exhibits, contemporary history unfolds in its political, social and cultural dimensions. There are short video films and vocal testimony is heard from life-sized figures of German chancellors, American presidents, even celebrities like Elvis Presley and Marilyn Monroe. The ultimate comment on the Nazi period comes from a huge statue of Charlie Chaplin in his role as the Great Dictator.

The **Städtische Galerie,** a municipal museum of 19th- and 20th-century art in the Lenbachhaus, boasts the largest collection of paintings by Wassily Kandinsky in Germany, plus important canvases by Franz Marc, August Macke and Paul Klee. The four formed the nucleus of Munich's pre-World War I "Blaue Reiter" (Blue Rider) school of painting. The name derives from a blue-and-black horseman drawn by Kandinsky for an almanac in 1912. Horses and the colour blue were also dominant features of Franz Marc's work.

In addition to Picasso, Braque, Dalí and the German Expressionists, the **Staatsgalerie moderner Kunst** collection (in the Haus der Kunst—see p. 59) includes a distinguished array of contemporary Americans.

GREATER MUNICH

Royal Retreats

Schloss Nymphenburg, now inside the ever-expanding city limits, was the Wittelsbachs' summer refuge from the heat of their Residenz in the city centre. The gleaming palace, with its spacious grounds, ponds, fountains and four enchanting garden pavilions, is a wonderful place to stroll and let your imagination go. Recall the *dolce far niente* of the Wittelsbachs' best days, when they played at nymphs and shepherds and forgot the worries of state. There's no U-Bahn station at the palace, but if you don't have a car for the 8-kilometre ride, a No. 12 tram will take you there from the Shiedplatz U-Bahn station.

The son and heir that Princess Henriette Adelaide presented to her husband in 1662 must have been an extraordinarily welcome gift. He was certainly an absolute boon to the architects of the time, inspiring the building of both the Theatinerkirche and Nymphenburg. The palace began modestly enough as a small summer villa, but it grew over the next century as each succeeding ruler added another wing or his own little pavilion and changed the landscaping of the gardens. Max Emanuel,

the little baby who was the cause of it all, grew up with the ambition of emulating Louis XIV's Versailles. He may not have succeeded completely, but the French armies appreciated his efforts and made Nymphenburg their headquarters in 1800.

The palace is approached by a long canal with avenues on either bank leading to a semicircle of lawns, the Schlossrondell, site of the building which houses the royal porcelain factory (see SHOPPING, p. 90). The central edifice of the palace proper contains galleries of superb 18th-century stucco work and ceiling frescoes. The majestic two-storey-high banqueting hall, known as **Steinerner Saal** (Stone Hall), has lively frescoes by Johann Baptist Zimmermann on the theme *Nymphen huldigen der Göttin Flora* (Nymphs Pay Homage to the Goddess Flora).

The first pavilion to the south holds the famous **Schönheitengalerie** (Gallery of Beautiful Women). Ludwig I commissioned Joseph Stieler to paint the portraits that hang here—a series of Munich's most beautiful young women.

Stroll back into another century in Nymphenburg gardens. Ludwig's coach awaits you in the Marstall.

The ferocious-looking lady with the belt of snakes around her waist and whip in hand, the notorious Lola Móntez, was probably his mistress. She was born Mary Dolores Eliza Rosanna Gilbert, daughter of an Irish adventurer. But since her mother was reputedly a Spanish countess, she went on stage as Señora Maria de los Dolores Porris y Móntez (see p. 22).

The **Marstallmuseum**—a dazzling collection of state coaches used for coronations, weddings and other royal frolics—has been installed in the south wing, in what was once the royal stables. From the extravagance of Karl Albrecht's 18th-century coronation coaches, the vehicles went on to achieve a state of ornamental delirium under Ludwig II. Note especially his Nymphenschlitten (Nymph sleigh), designed for escapades in the foothills of the Alps.

The **gardens** were originally laid out in a subdued Italian style for Henriette Adelaide, but her son preferred the grandiose French manner. Later, Ludwig von Sckell, landscape artist of the Englischer Garten, was brought in. As a result, the park has lost some of its formality, which makes for a more relaxed stroll. But by the same token, the Baroque and Rococo pavilions seem a little isolated now, like original tenants who stayed on in the house while new owners changed all the furniture around them. Traces of the former classical geometry can be seen in the symmetry of the Schlossrondell and the rectangular Grosses Parterre immediately west of the central edifice. The grounds are decorated with some rather nice marble statues of Greek gods by Dominikus Auliczek and others.

Off to the left lies **Amalienburg,** known as one of the most beautiful rococo rooms in Germany. It was begun in 1734 by the same trio who worked on the State Rooms of the Residenz—architect François de Cuvilliés, sculptor Joachim Dietrich and stucco artist Johann Baptist Zimmermann. Wander through the rooms where the hunting dogs and rifles were kept, the Pheasant Room next to the blue-and-white, Dutch-tiled kitchen, and, above all, the brilliant silver and pastel yellow Rococo **Spiegelsaal** (Hall of Mirrors). This was originally—just imagine—the pavilion's entrance.

Continue west to the **Badenburg** (Bath Pavilion)—fitted

with Delft china fixtures that are an interior decorator's dream—and the Grosser See, a large pond dotted with islands. Overlooking it is a promontory with a little love temple modelled after Rome's Temple of Vesta, goddess of fire.

North of the central canal with its spectacular **cascade** of water is another, smaller pond. On the far side stands the **Pagodenburg,** an octagonal tea pavilion with some exotic black-and-red-lacquered Chinese chambers upstairs.

The fourth of the park's pavilions, the **Magdalenenklause** (Hermitage) was built in 1725 for the private meditations of Max Emanuel. The dominant theme of the paintings and sculptures inside is penitence. Don't be surprised when you see that the building is a crumbling ruin; cracks and flaking plaster were deliberately incorporated in the mock Romanesque and Gothic structure, not to mention the Moorish minaret thrown in for good measure.

The area north of the park has been given over to the **Neuer Botanischer Garten** (New Botanical Gardens), entered from Menzinger Strasse. The Arboretum at the west end of the gardens is cleverly landscaped to resemble different climatic regions of the world with their appropriate flora—pine forest, Arctic tundra, heath and moorland, desert dunes, the steppes and Alpine country alongside an artificial pond.

After the flamboyance of Nymphenburg, continue further west (by car or No. 73 tram from the end of Menzinger Strasse) to the refreshing simplicity of **Schloss Blutenburg,** now a convent. It's particularly worth visiting for the **palace chapel,** of a superb Late Gothic type rare in this part of Bavaria. The three altars display splendid paintings by Jan Polack, done in 1491: the *Holy Trinity* (high altar), *Christ Enthroned* (on the left) and the *Annunciation* (to the right). On the walls are fine polychrome wooden sculptures of the Apostles, Mary and a resurrected Christ, dated around 1500.

Finish your tour in nearby Pippinger Strasse with a visit to **Pfarrkirche St. Wolfgang** (St. Wolfgang's Parish Church). Some frescoes attributed to Polack (1479) decorate the admirably serene interior and there are three delicately carved wooden altars from the same period. The church offers perfect meditation at the end of a long day.

Excursions

To take the full measure of Munich, you must visit its hinterland, the beautiful countryside of Bavaria. Go to the lakes, to the little country churches and to Ludwig II's crazy castles. If you don't have a car, take one of the tours organized by the Munich-Upper Bavaria Tourist Office (see p. 123). Each tour we propose can be done easily in one day.

Ludwig's Follies

Ludwig II's castles south of Munich, Neuschwanstein and Linderhof, are best visited separately. Choose one, or, if you're a real fan, do both.

Take the A 99 and B 12 to **Landsberg am Lech** (interesting medieval town centre), then the B 17, the Deutsche Alpenstrasse (German Alpine Road). Stop off at STEINGADEN to visit the beautiful **St. Johann Baptist Church,** which retains much of its 12th-century Romanesque exterior. You'll enjoy the pleasant walk in the old cloister.

It's worth making a detour to the east to visit the magnificent **Wieskirche,** a pilgrimage church of 1754 designed by Dominikus Zimmermann

Neuschwanstein was one of Ludwig II's grander little whims. Kings no longer have dreams like this.

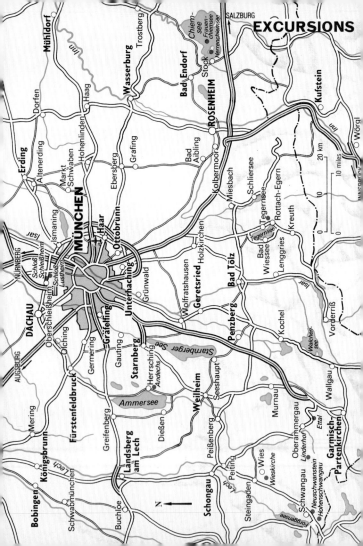

EXCURSIONS

and decorated with a sublime ceiling fresco by his brother Johann Baptist, depicting Christ dispensing divine mercy. In its architecture and decoration, the church is a consummate work, perfect to the last Rococo detail.

Return to the main road for the journey down to the more pagan inspiration of **Neuschwanstein.** After visiting the medieval castle of Wartburg in Thuringia in 1867, Ludwig's imagination was fired with a vision of the Minnesänger—minstrels of the 12th century—and he decided to build a castle that would recapture the aura of that romantic era.

Ludwig replaced a ruined mountain retreat of his father's in the Schwangau with an extraordinary white-turreted castle. Set in the middle of a forest of firs and pines, it overlooks the gorge of Pöllat and Lake Forggen. Visit the great dreamer's throne room and imagine, as did Ludwig, the minstrel contests of another age in the Sängersaal. Wagnerians will recognize the sculptural and painted allusions to *Tannhäuser, The Mastersingers of Nuremberg* and *Tristan and Isolde.*

While Neuschwanstein was under construction, Ludwig kept an eye on progress from the nearby castle of **Hohenschwangau** (just 1 kilometre away), a neo-Gothic building put up by his father, Maximilian II. In fact, Neuschwanstein and Hohenschwangau are known collectively as "die Königsschlösser". Take a look at the music room, with its display of Wagner memorabilia (the composer stayed at Hohenschwangau) and Ludwig's bedroom, noted for its star-studded ceiling.

To reach Ludwig's second dream castle, take the Garmisch-Partenkirchen Autobahn from Munich, turning off west to **Ettal.** Set in a gently curving valley is a lovely Benedictine monastery with a fine domed church. Stop to admire Johann Jakob Zeiller's 18th-century fresco of the life of St. Benedict. Then go on to **Oberammergau,** site of the famous ten-yearly Passion Play inaugurated in the plague year of 1633. The town preserves some very attractive 18th-century house façades painted by the so-called *Lüftlmaler* (air painter), Franz Zwinck. The best are Pilatushaus and Geroldhaus.

Linderhof, Ludwig's favourite castle, was the embodiment of his most Baroque fantasies. The palace, inspired by the Grand Trianon of Versailles, is **81**

opulent inside and out. Quite apart from the carefully tailored landscape of pond and park, you could be excused for believing that the whole romantic Alpine backdrop of the Graswangtal had been conjured up from Ludwig's imagination. But the Venus Grotto, carved out of the mountainside with another Wagnerian motif from *Tannhäuser*, is man-made.

The Lakes

Ammersee (35 km. south-west of Munich on the B 12) is a delightful place for long walks along the lake or up into the wooded hills around it. Make for the Benedictine **Abbey of Andechs** in the hills that overlook Ammersee from the east. The church was put up in the 15th century and was redecorated in the Rococo style by Johann Baptist Zimmermann, then at the peak of his career. The monastery brewery produces first-rate beer.

Starnberger See (take the S-Bahn or Garmisch-Partenkirchen Autobahn south-west) offers quiet, rural scenery and a peaceful rush-fringed shoreline. It was here that Ludwig II drowned in 1886 (see p. 24). He had been held in custody at Schloss Berg, near the resort town of STARNBERG.

Tegernsee (Salzburg Autobahn, Holzkirchen exit) was once a focal point of German culture, dating back to the 8th century. Its monastery was a magnet for church intellectuals, who drew on a library that in 1500 was bigger than the Vatican's. With the French Revolution came secularization and the removal of the monastery's treasures to Munich. Today the Benedictine Abbey houses a beer hall, and Tegernsee ranks as a high centre of German social life. The élite of Munich society congregate around the lake, partaking of the iodised waters at BAD WIESSEE and dining out in ROTTACH. Join them.

Chiemsee (south-east of Munich on the Salzburg Autobahn) is the largest of the Bavarian lakes and the site of Ludwig II's most ambitious castle. **Herrenchiemsee** stands on an island, the Herreninsel, at the western end of the lake. (You take a boat from the jetty at STOCK.)

Ludwig started his last big castle in 1878 but ran out of money—and time—in 1886.

If you've seen enough monasteries, Andechs is worth it for the beer.

theatres of Schwabing specialize in a more avant-garde repertoire, as does the open-air theatre at Olympiapark. For children—and adults—there are two wonderful theatres: the Puppentheater (Glove-puppet Theatre) in the Künstlerhaus on Lenbachplatz, and the Marionettentheater, Blumenstrasse 29 a, near Sendlinger Tor, with shows for children in the afternoon and marionette opera for adults in the evening.

For those with an interest in the honourable tradition of **political cabaret,** Schwabing is still the place to go to. Most of the troupes have the longevity of butterflies, but the best-established are the Münchner Lach- und Schiessgesellschaft (Ursulastrasse 9) and the Münchner Rationaltheater (Hesseloher Strasse 18).

More conventional **nightclubs** and **discothèques** are to be found in the centre of town and in Schwabing, but **beer halls** still provide the most relaxed night-time entertainment.

And then there is the delightful Hellabrunn **Zoo** (U3 underground to Thalkirchen from Marienplatz). Animals are grouped according to their continent of origin—Europe, Africa, Asia, America, Australia and the polar regions. Here you'll see such zoological curiosities as the tarpan, a kind of horse, and the white-tailed gnu. The antics of the chimps "working out" in their own private gym always attract an appreciative audience.

Festivals

The people of Munich always have something to celebrate. Over a hundred days a year are officially devoted to festivals, processions, banquets and street dances commemorating events like the arrival of the first strong beer of the year *(Starkbierzeit)* or the departure—several centuries ago!—of this plague or that occupying army. Any excuse will do.

Fasching (carnival) is almost as mad in Munich as in the Rhineland. It runs from January 7. Some 2,500 balls are held all over town for policemen and doctors, lawyers and butchers, artists and plumbers. There are masked processions and market women at the Viktualienmarkt have their fling at midday on Shrove Tuesday.

Loud, joyous and full of rhythm, Bavarian music keeps you young.

The biggest blow-out of all, of course, is the **Oktoberfest.** Not many people remember that this binge began with the marriage of Crown Prince Ludwig (later Ludwig I) to Princess Theresa in 1810. The wedding was celebrated in October with a horse race and everybody came. They came again the next year, and the year after that, and they're still coming.

The horse race has been dropped and the festivities now take place during the warmer second half of September, but the blushing bride is remembered in the name of the Oktoberfest site—Theresienwiese. Locals, however, refer to it as the "Wies'n", a nickname for the actual festival, too. During the two weeks of Oktoberfest, revellers consume gargantuan quantities of beer, toted around ten litres at a time by hefty beermaids. The brew washes down hundreds of thousands of barbecued chickens, while the operator of a monster roasting spit boasts that he turns out up to 60 whole oxen during the festival. And to work all that off, there's the fun of the fair: roller-coasters, giant ferris-wheel, dodg'em cars. Or to scare it off, Schichtl's age-old horror show.

Shopping

Munich is an elegant town, capital of Germany's fashion industry, so there's no lack of chic boutiques, especially on Theatinerstrasse, Maximilianstrasse and Schwabing's Leopoldstrasse. You'll also find the world's best selection of well-tailored garments (coats, jackets and suits) in **Loden** cloth, a Bavarian speciality. Originally developed for hunters, this waterproof wool fabric in navy, grey or traditional green has kept the people of Munich warm in winter for over a hundred years.

You might even care to try the local Bavarian costume *(Tracht)*. There are smart green-collared grey jackets for men or, for women, gaily coloured dirndl dresses with a full gathered skirt and fitted bodice.

German **leather** and **sportswear** are good buys. And Lederhosen, those slap-happy shorts for Bavarians, may amuse the children.

Nymphenburg **porcelain** is still turned out in traditional Rococo designs. View pieces at the Nymphenburger Schlossrondell factory (see p. 74). Connoisseurs should be on the look-out for old Meissen or modern Rosenthal.

German **cutlery,** kitchen utensils and **electronic gadgets** are of a very high standard and superbly designed. You might also like to consider **linens** with modern or traditional designs, noted for their good old-fashioned quality. The best bet is a sumptuous duck- or goose-down *Feder-bett*—a good way to save on winter heating bills.

Many people appreciate German **binoculars** and **tele-scopes.** And, while the competition from Japan is keen, there are still many fine **came-ras** on the market, especially at the miniature end of the range. Germany has always pro-

If you like hats, the whimsical creations of Munich's milliners will almost certainly tickle your fancy.

duced excellent children's **toys** and its industrial prowess is reflected in the intricate building sets and model trains.

The presence of so many great orchestras and musicians in Germany means that the selection of **records** here is probably second only to the United States. The manufacture of **musical instruments,** including the finest grand pianos, violins—even harmonicas —enjoys a venerable reputation.

91

Quite apart from the posh shops in the city centre, you should keep your eyes open for **flea markets.** They pop up all over Schwabing whenever students and artists run out of rent money. But the best are the seasonal ones known as "Auer Dult", which date back to the 14th century. These are held for eight days, three times a year (May, July and October) in the Au district (around Mariahilfplatz south of the Deutsches Museum). You can tell that these markets turn out interesting bargains by the number of city-centre antique dealers on the spot early in the morning. Just beat them to it.

Sports

The city's great boon to sports lovers was the construction of the Olympic facilities in 1972 (see p. 56). The Municipal Sports Office (Städtisches Sportamt) can provide information about the daily programme of events and training at the Olympic Stadium's Gesundheitspark (Health Park). Visitors and regulars alike can participate.

Anyone can use the **swimming pool** at the Olympia Schwimmhalle, in addition to eight other indoor and ten open-air pools around town. The latter all provide lawns for

sunbathing. Year-round, **ice-skating** fans congregate at the Olympic ice rink and speed-skating track.

Munich has its share of **tennis** courts, too: the best are at Olympiapark, in the Englischer Garten and, most attractive of all, at Schloss Nymphenburg.

While real "runners" will want to work out in the stadium, lesser mortals will be content **jogging** in the Englischer Garten, especially the stretch along the River Isar.

Or try **cycling** the 9-mile river path to Ismaning. **Golf** courses are to be found in outlying Strasslach and in Thalkirchen, on the south-west edge of town.

For people who don't want to exert themselves, delightful **raft trips** *(Flossfahrten)* are organized at weekends. You drift down the Isar from Wolfratshausen to Munich, while the beer flows and brass bands play.

Spectator sports are dominated by **soccer,** for one of the

Look hard enough and you'll find the strangest birds at local flea markets. Try sailing on the Starnberger See—or dream about it.

best teams in Europe, Bayern München (Bayern Munich), plays at the Olympic Stadium. Rowing and canoeing events are held at Schloss Schleissheim. East of the city centre, you can watch horseracing at Riem or trotting at Daglfing.

Further out of Munich, you can get down to serious **sailing** or **windsurfing** on the Ammersee, Starnberger See and Tegernsee. The lakes and rivers also offer good **fishing.**

For deer and wild boar **hunting** in the Bavarian forests, apply for a licence to the German Hunting Association (Deutscher Jagdschutzverband, J. Henrystrasse 26, Bonn 1). **Hiking** is a major pastime, especially as you approach the Bavarian Alps. Just 97 kilometres from Munich, Garmisch-Partenkirchen, the principal resort, provides guides for **mountain climbing.** There are plenty of peaks to tackle, including the 9,721-foot Zugspitze.

Once you're in the Alps, all the **winter sports** are at your disposal. In addition to skiing (and a very professional ski school), Garmisch has its own Olympic rink for skating and ice hockey. For the more sedate, there's curling; for the less constrained, a bobsleigh run.

Dining Out

Eating and drinking in Bavaria in general, and in Munich in particular, are major occupations. Conviviality reigns supreme, both in the high temples of gastronomy and at the long, communal tables of the Bräuhaus and Gaststätte*.

Meal Times

Lunch (*Mittagessen*) is usually served from 11.30 a.m. to 2 p.m., dinner (*Abendessen*) from 6.30 to 8.30 (to 10.30 or 11 in large establishments). Most Germans like to eat their main meal in the middle of the day. They generally prefer a light supper (*Abendbrot,* or "evening bread") at night, consisting of cold meats and cheeses with the possible addition of a salad.

Where to Eat

With its great prosperity and tradition of good living, Munich has more refined *Restaurants* than might be expected by those who pre-judge German cuisine as heavy and unimaginative. Most of them are situated in Maximilianstrasse, Residenzstrasse and Theati-

---

* For a comprehensive guide to dining out in Germany, consult the Berlitz EUROPEAN MENU READER.

nerstrasse, along Schwabing's Leopoldstrasse and in Prinzregentenstrasse at the southern end of the Englischer Garten. Some of the better establishments are combined with high-quality delicatessens.

Munich's growing sophistication is such that elegance, however casual, is more important than the old formality of ties for men or skirts for women. It's a good idea to reserve in advance at the smarter places. Service (15%) is already included in the bill, but no one has ever been known to refuse a little extra.

Niceties of dress and advance reservations are not a problem at the more popular *Gaststätte* or *Bräuhaus*, literally "brewery", but actually a beer hall. These establishments usually serve full meals as well as beer, though not always in every section of the bigger halls. All the great breweries operate their own beer halls in Munich, and beer gardens, too, many of them with brass bands. In the inner city, the beer halls also have an open-air *Biergarten*. The Englischer Garten's popular beer gardens are to be found at the Chinese Tower, at the Hirschau and beside the Kleinhesseloher See.

Weinstuben (taverns), less numerous in the beer country of Bavaria than in other regions of Germany, serve open wine by the glass—rather than by the carafe or bottle. Taverns also provide meals.

In a separate category is the *Konditorei* (café-cum-pastry shop), the bourgeois fairyland where you can spend a whole afternoon reading newspapers attached to rods. This is just the place to stuff yourself with pastry, ice-cream, coffee, tea and fruit juices, even a good selection of wines. Most provide a limited selection of egg dishes, light snacks and salads.

Local Customs

In a Gaststätte or Bräuhaus, you'll sometimes come across a sign on one of the long tables proclaiming *"Stammtisch"*. This means the seats have been reserved for regulars—club, firm or big family. It is otherwise customary for strangers to sit together, usually with a polite query as to whether one of the six or seven empty places is *"frei"*. Fellow diners usually wish each other *"Mahlzeit"* or *"Guten Appetit"*.

It may come as a surprise that each bread roll *(Semmel)* is charged separately; you're expected to keep a count of how many you've eaten.

But we mustn't forget Munich's myriad ethnic restaurants: French, Italian, Greek and Balkan. The city also has its quota of fast-food chains.

Breakfast *(Frühstück)*
Germans start the day with a meal that is somewhat more substantial than the typical "Continental" breakfast. The distinctive touch is the selection of cold meats—ham, salami and liver sausage (liverwurst)—and cheese served with the bread. Not just one kind of bread, but brown (rye with caraway seeds), rich black (pumpernickel) and white. If you like boiled eggs, try *Eier im Glas*, two four-minute eggs served whole, already shelled, in a glass dish. Gone the problem of whether to crumble or guillotine the top of your eggshell. And with it all comes tea, hot chocolate or coffee that's stronger than the Anglo-American brew, but weaker than the French or Italian.

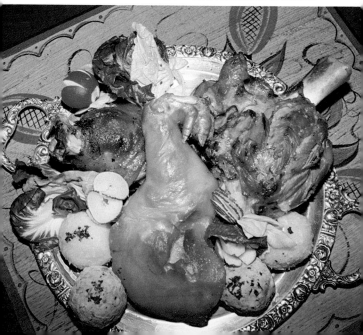

Soups and Starters

Bavarians make excellent *Leberknödlsuppe*, a soup with spicy dumplings of flour, bread crumbs, beef liver, onions, marjoram and garlic. *Kartoffelsuppe* contains potato, celery, leek and parsnip. Other soups are made with beans *(Bohnensuppe)* or lentils *(Linsensuppe)*, often with pieces of sausage.

If you prefer an hors d'œuvre to a soup, try smoked calf's tongue served with a little horseradish sauce *(Kalbszüngerl)* or pork tongue boiled with juniper berries, bay leaves and peppercorns, accompanied by a small portion of sauerkraut *(Schweinszüngerl im Kraut)*.

Bavarian Specialities

The pig and the calf dominate Bavarian main dishes, often in combination. Pork or veal can be either pot-roasted (*Kalbs-* or *Schweinsbraten*) or grilled on a spit (*Kalbs-* or *Schweinshaxen*) with a marvellous crispy, crackling skin. The ultimate in delicious roasts is *Spanferkel*, suckling pig.

Bavarian food is rich, whether it be suckling pig or chocolate cake.

For a royal change, sample the excellent game when in season—venison, hare, partridge and pheasant. The venison is usually carefully marinated till tender and served with sweet raisin or redcurrant sauce or a purée of chestnuts. The best of the local freshwater fish are trout *(Forelle),* **97**

unbeatable when boiled absolutely fresh *(blau)*, or whitefish *(Renke)*, usually fried.

Accompanying it all is a crisp, green salad or those Bavarian staples, the potato and the cabbage. Choose an old stand-by like sautéed potatoes *(Bratkartoffeln)* or the excellent potato salad *(Kartoffelsalat)*. Cabbage of course means *Sauerkraut*, often beautifully prepared in white wine with juniper berries, caraway seeds and cloves. But there's also the sweet-and-sour red cabbage, *Blaukraut*, done with apples, raisins and white vinegar, or a good green cabbage salad *(Weisskrautsalat)*.

Snacks

Given the importance of beer-drinking in Munich's social life, snacks *(Schmankerl)* are correspondingly important to aid and abet a thirst for beer. Also to keep drinkers "afloat", so to speak. You eat them at any time of day.

Local people favour sausages of all kinds as a snack food. Pork and veal join forces in the *Weisswürste* (white sausages), flavoured with pepper, parsley and onions. The best establishments—and in this case we mean the most observant of traditional standards—never serve *Weisswürste* in the afternoon. They're no longer fresh enough for the discerning palate, i.e. a Bavarian. *Bratwurst*, another sausage staple, is made of pork and grilled or sautéed. The best are the little ones sent down fraternally from Nuremberg. You may also enjoy the spicy *Blutwurst* (blood sausage) or *Leberwurst* (liver sausage or liverwurst).

You should also be on the look-out for a delicious but misleading snack called *Leberkäs*. Literally, this means "liver-cheese", but has neither liver nor cheese in it, being rather a mixture of pork, bacon and beef, spiced with nutmeg, marjoram and onions and eaten hot or cold. Other great snacks include: *Reiberdatschi*, deep-fried potato pancakes; *Obatzta*, a spicy mixture of creamy cheeses with chives, paprika, caraway seeds, salt and pepper; and thin slices of horseradish *(Radi)*.

Failing any of these, stimulate your thirst with the salty pretzels *(Bretzel)*.

Desserts

Apart from a couple of regional variations on apple cake *(Apfelkücherl)*, and plum cake *(Zwetschgendatschi)*, Bavarians are quite happy to join in the national orgy of Konditorei pastries *Schwarzwälder Kirschtorte*, the cherry cake from the Black Forest and *Apfelstrudel* from Vienna are very welcome treats.

Wines

Bavaria stopped making good wine centuries ago, but Munich restaurants offer an excellent array of Rhine and Mosel wines, mostly white. Here's a guide to the best German vintages:

The most highly reputed Rhine wines are those of the Rheingau, the pick of the crop being *Schloss Johannisberger, Hattenheimer, Kloster Eberbacher* and *Rüdesheimer*. The next best come from the more southerly vineyards, the famous *Liebfraumilch, Niersteiner, Domtal* and *Oppenheimer*. Next in quality are the Mittelrhein wines from Bingen, Bacharach, Boppard and Oberwesel.

The Mosel wines, bottled in green glass to distinguish them from the brown Rhine bottles, enjoy a delicate reputation through the fame of the *Bernkasteler, Piesporter* and *Zeltinger*.

Germany also produces a very respectable sparkling, champagne-like wine called *Sekt*, from the Rheingau region of Eltville and Hochheim.

(The latter provides the English gentleman with his all-purpose name for German white wines, "hock".)

Beer

Bavarians appreciate the old saying that there's good beer and better beer, but there's no bad beer. Not in Bavaria.

Beer *vom Fass* (on tap) can be ordered by the half-litre in restaurants, but elsewhere often only in a one-litre tankard known as the *Masskrug* or simply *"Mass"*. Bottled beer comes in several varieties: *Export*, light and smooth; *Pils*, light and strong; and *Bock*, dark and rich.

Bavarian beer is generally lighter than other German beers, but it has its strong forms, too. If you like it dark with a slightly sweet, malt flavour, order *Dunkles*. This is not served as cold as the more popular light lager brew, *Helles,* with an inviting mist on the glass.

Other Drinks

If you just want to be refreshed, rather than stimulated, you'll find an unusually wide assortment of fruit juices, the best being *Johannisbeersaft* (red- or blackcurrant), *Apfelsaft* (apple) and *Traubensaft* (grape—non-alcoholic). **99**

Keeping It Flowing

Most of the time, there are enough big festivals to keep the beer flowing steadily down the Bavarian gullet. But Munich brewers can't bear slack periods.

In the third and fourth weeks before Easter, the so-called *Starkbierzeit* (Strong-beer Time), they stage beer festivals to promote their *Märzenbier* (March Ale). After Easter comes the *Maibockzeit*, when they push the strong dark stuff. In the summer, everybody's thirsty enough not to need too much prompting.

Then comes the Oktoberfest (see p. 90), the ultimate in beer festivals, when every brewery participates in a colourful parade of horse-drawn wagons. Christmas and Fasching (carnival) tide the poor brewers over till it's time again for *Märzenbier*. In Munich every day's a holiday for beer.

To Help You Order...

Could I/we have a table? **Ich hätte/Wir hatten gerne einen Tisch.**

Waiter/waitress, please! **Ober/Fräulein, bitte.**

The check, please. **Zahlen, bitte.**

I would like... **Ich möchte gerne...**

beer	**ein Bier**	menu	**die Karte**
bread	**etwas Brot**	milk	**Milch**
butter	**etwas Butter**	mineral water	**Mineralwasser**
cheese	**Käse**	mustard	**etwas Senf**
coffee	**einen Kaffee**	potatoes	**Kartoffeln**
cold cuts	**Aufschnitt**	saccharin	**Süssstoff**
dessert	**eine Nachspeise**	salad	**Salat**
eggs	**Eier**	salt	**Salz**
fish	**Fisch**	soup	**eine Suppe**
fruit	**Obst**	sugar	**Zucker**
hors d'œuvre	**eine Vorspeise**	tea	**einen Tee**
ice-cream	**Eiskrem**	vegetables	**Gemüse**
lemon	**Zitrone**	whipped cream	**Schlagsahne**
meat	**Fleisch**	wine	**Wein**

...and Read the Menu

Apfel	apple	**Lachs**	salmon
Blumenkohl	cauliflower	**Lamm**	lamb
Bohnen	green beans	**Nierchen**	kidneys
Braten	roast beef	**Nudeln**	noodles
Ente	duck	**Pilze**	mushrooms
Erdbeeren	strawberries	**Radi/Kren**	horse-radish
Geselchtes	smoked meat	**Reis**	rice
Gurkensalat	cucumber salad	**Rindfleisch**	beef
Hühnchen	chicken	**Rippchen**	smoked pork chops
Jägerschnitzel	cutlet with mushroom sauce	**Rollmops**	marinated herring
Kalbfleisch	veal	**Schinken**	ham
Klösse	dumplings	**Schweinefleisch**	pork
Kraut	cabbage	**Spargel**	asparagus
Kraftbrühe	bouillon	**Wild**	game
Krautwickerl	stuffed cabbage	**Wurst**	sausage
Kuchen	cake	**Zwiebeln**	onions

101

BLUEPRINT for a Perfect Trip

How to Get There

Because of the complexity and variability of the many fares, you should ask the advice of an informed travel agent well before departure.

BY AIR

Scheduled flights

Munich airport (see also p. 107) is served by many European and some intercontinental flights. However, the main airport for transatlantic flights is Frankfurt, from where there are about 15 flights a day to Munich, leaving every half-hour. Average journey time from London to Munich is 1½ hours, from New York 9 hours.

Charter flights and package tours

From the U. K. and Ireland: A variety of combinations is offered for stays of a weekend to six nights or longer. Many tours include accommodation, breakfast, sightseeing tours of the city or nearby towns and free admission to museums and galleries in Munich. Budget packages are available from the Munich tourist office under the "Key to Munich" scheme. Contact any travel agency or the tourist office itself (see pp. 122–23).

From North America: Several packages to Germany and Austria feature Munich. These all-inclusive tours provide transport, hotel accommodation, tranfers, baggage handling, taxes and tips, meals as specified in each itinerary, some or all sightseeing and the services of an English-speaking guide.

BY ROAD

Munich can be reached by motorway (expressway) from nearly anywhere in Europe (Brussels–Munich 815 km./505 miles, Basle 394 km./244 miles, Hamburg 795 km./493 miles). If you don't want to drive on the *autobahn,* but would like to enjoy the nature and culture along the way, you can contact your automobile association and get help to plan a suitable route. Those not in a rush might like to follow the Rhine from Koblenz down to Mainz, for some of Germany's most pleasurable scenery, before branching off on the autobahn No. 3 as far as Nuremberg, then the No. 9 to Munich.

Numerous tour operators in Germany and abroad offer **coach tours** to Munich all year round. Reservations must be booked in advance. The journey from London to Munich direct takes approximately 24 hours.

BY RAIL

Potential rail travellers will find information on trains and reduced-price tickets on pp. 124–125. There are numerous trains a day from

London to Munich via Dover and Ostend, a journey of 17 hours. The service via Harwich and the Hook of Holland (20 hours) is direct, but passengers on the night train must change in Cologne. In the season there's a *Train Auto Couchettes* from Paris to Munich. Seats or sleepers should be booked well in advance.

When you book your train, you might think of the **rail/road** possibility, where you pick up a rental car at the station on arrival.

When to Go

Whatever the season, Munich has something to offer the visitor. There are, of course, the well-publicized Oktoberfest celebrations in late September and the revelry of Fasching (Carnival) in January/February. But Munich has many attractions more, from the superb collections of the Alte Pinakothek and Residenzmuseum to the abundance of fine shops and restaurants in streets like Theatinerstrasse. Music events are scheduled year-round, including an international film festival during the last week of June and the Münchner Festspiele in July and August. No matter when you visit the capital of Bavaria, there's always a great deal to see and do.

The following chart shows Munich's average daytime temperatures:

	J	F	M	A	M	J	J	A	S	O	N	D
°F	34	37	48	57	64	70	73	73	68	55	45	35
°C	1	3	9	14	18	21	23	23	20	13	7	2

Planning Your Budget

To give you an idea of what to expect, here's a list of average prices in marks (DM). They can only be approximate, however, as even in Germany inflation creeps relentlessly up.

Airport transfer. S-Bahn line 8 to central railway station DM 10, bus 12, taxi DM 100.

Baby-sitters. DM 12–15 per hour.

Camping. DM 25–30 for two persons with car and tent or caravan trailer).

Car hire. *Ford Escort* DM 219 per day, DM 800 per week with unlimited mileage. *Opel Vectra* DM 299 per day. *BMW 520* DM 425 per day, all with unlimited mileage. Tax included, special prices for weekends.

Cigarettes. DM 4,20 per packet of 19.

Entertainment. Cinema DM 9–11, theatre DM 25–50, discotheques and nightclubs entrance usually free.

Hairdressers. *Woman's* haircut DM 55, shampoo and set DM 50, blow-dry DM 55, permanent wave DM 100. *Man's* haircut DM 45.

Hotels (double room per night). Luxury class DM 300–600, first class DM 230–440, medium class DM 180–335, budget class DM 115–180. *Boarding house* DM 75–150.

Meals and drinks. Continental breakfast DM 15, lunch or dinner in fairly good establishment DM 25–50, bottle of wine (German) DM 30–40, beer (small bottle) DM 5, soft drinks (small bottle) DM 3, coffee DM 3.

Museums. DM 3–8.

Shopping bag. 1 kg. of bread DM 5,50, 250 g. of butter DM 2.50, 6 eggs DM 1.80, 1 kg. of hamburger meat DM 25, ½ kg. of coffee DM 8, 100 g. of instant coffee DM 6.50, ½ litre of beer DM 1.20, 1 litre of soft drink DM 1.20.

Taxis. Initial charge DM 3.90, plus DM 2.20 per km within centre of Munich.

Youth hostels. Youth hostel six-bed rooms) DM 36 per person, breakfast included.

An A–Z Summary of Practical Information and Facts

Listed after many entries is the appropriate German translation, usually in the singular, plus a number of phrases that should help you when seeking assistance.

A   **ACCOMMODATION.** See also CAMPING. The Munich tourist offices provide a free multi-lingual list with full details of amenities and prices of accommodation in the city. They also operate a hotel-booking service at the airport and at the central railway station (no telephone calls) for a small charge; note that part of the room rate must be paid in advance. For a wider selection, consult the *German Hotel Guide*, distributed free by the German National Tourist Board (see TOURIST INFORMATION OFFICES). During the summer, at week-ends and in periods with special events, it is advisable to book well ahead. The Allgemeine Deutsche Zimmerreservierung (ADZ) operates a computer reservation system at:

Beethovenstrasse 61, D-6000 Frankfurt am Main: tel. (069) 74 07 67

In addition to hotels, there are inns *(Gasthof)* and boarding houses *(Pension)*. The tourist office can arrange for accommodation in private homes—a nice way to get to know the local people. If you are touring Bavaria by car, look out for "Zimmer frei" (room to let) signs.

A list of hotels and inns in Upper Bavaria is available from Fremdenverkehrsverband München-Oberbayern:

Sonnenstrasse 10/III, D-8000 München 2; tel. (089) 59 73 47/48; fax 59 31 87

Youth hostels. If you are planning to make extensive use of youth hostels during your stay in Munich, obtain an international membership card from your national youth hostel association before departure. For full information about hostels in West Germany, contact the German Youth Hostel Association *(Deutsches Jugendherbergswerk—DJH):*

Bülowstrasse 26, D-4930 Detmold

The above-mentioned organization maintains the following hostels in and around Munich:

DJH München 19, Wendl-Dietrich-Strasse 20; tel. 13 11 56
Jugendgästehaus Thalkirchen, Miesingstrasse 4; tel. 723 65 60
Jugendherberge Burg Schwaneck, Burgweg 4–6, D-8023 Pullach; tel. 793 06 43

Further possibilities:

Christlicher Verein Junger Männer (YMCA), Landwehrstrasse 13;
tel. 552 14 10
Haus International, Elisabethstrasse 87 (Schwabing);
tel. 12 00 60

I'd like a single room/double room.	**Ich hätte gern ein Einzelzimmer/ Doppelzimmer.**
with bath/shower	**mit Bad/Dusche**
What's the rate per night/week?	**Wieviel kostet es pro Nacht/ Woche?**

AIRPORT *(Flughafen).* Airport München II, about 30 kilometres east of the city centre, handles domestic and international flights. You will find banks, car hire desks, restaurants, coffee bars, news- and souvenir-stands, a post office, hairdresser, hotel reservation desk, tourist information offices and duty-free shops.

Ground transport. Taxis and suburban trains *(S-Bahn)* shuttle between the airport and the main railway station *(Hauptbahnhof).* By S-Bahn, you can travel from Pasing on the recently opened S8 line directly to the airport arrival hall. The journey takes about 38 minutes, and trains leave every 20 minutes. Buses leave Arnulfstrasse outside the main railway station every 20 minutes from 3.10 a.m. until 9.30 p.m. and run from the airport between 6.25 a.m. and 0.25 a.m. Buses also stop at the Kieferngarten Underground station. However, buses are sometimes unreliable due to traffic jams on the motorway.

Airport information, tel. 921 22 11

Lufthansa (Germany's national airline) reservation desks can be reached by dialling 5 11 38.

BICYCLE HIRE *(Fahrradverleih).* Nowadays, cyclists are well catered for, with a network of bicycle-only lanes covering some 200 kilometres in and around the city centre. The tourist office can supply names of cycle-hire firms.

It's also pleasant to tour the countryside around Munich by bike. Many train and S-Bahn stations in the small outlying towns and villages provide a year-round bicycle hire service. A list of participating stations *(Fahrradbahnhof)* is available at ticket counters and tourist offices. In some places, you can hire a bicycle at one station and return it to another. Suggested itineraries are indicated on notice boards at

B the stations. Railway passengers hiring bikes are entitled to a special discount.

Are there bicycles for hire at this station?	**Kann man an diesem Bahnhof Fahrräder mieten?**
May I return it to another station?	**Kann ich es an einem anderen Bahnhof zurückgeben?**

C **CAMPING.** Four major campsites are situated within the city limits:

Langwieder See, Eschenrieder Strasse 119 (north-west, along the Augsburg–Stuttgart motorway), open April 1–mid-October (tel. 8141566).

Campingplatz München-**Ludwigsfeld,** Dachauer Strasse 571 (north-west, on the road to Dachau), open year-round (tel. 1506936).

München-**Obermenzing,** Lochhausener Strasse 59 (north-west, along the Augsburg–Stuttgart motorway), open mid-March–early November (tel. 8112235).

Campingplatz München-**Thalkirchen,** Zentralländstrasse 49 (on the Isar river, opposite the Zoo), open mid-March–end-October (tel. 7231707).

From the end of June through August, the city of Munich runs a campsite for youths, **Jugendlager Kapuzinerhölzl,** at Franz-Schrank-Strasse. A tent large enough for 300 people is set up; bring a sleeping bag and air mattress.

Sites are indicated by the international blue sign with a black tent on a white background. Some sites give reductions to members of the International Camping Association.

For full information about sites and facilities, consult the guides published by the German Automobile Club ADAC or the German Camping Club *(Deutscher Camping-Club—DCC):*

Mandlstrasse 28, D - 8000 München 40; tel. (089) 334021

If you camp off the beaten track, be sure to obtain the permission of the proprietor or the police, and note that camping in the rest-areas off the motorways is not permitted.

May we camp here?	**Dürfen wir hier zelten?**
Is there a campsite nearby?	**Gibt es in der Nähe einen Zeltplatz?**

CAR HIRE *(Autovermietung).* See also DRIVING. You can arrange to hire a car immediately upon arrival at Munich's airport or central railway station. Otherwise enquire at your hotel or refer to the yellow pages of the telephone directory for addresses of leading firms. It's usually possible to have a car delivered to your hotel if you wish. Larger firms allow you to return cars to another European city for an extra fee. Special weekend and weekly unlimited mileage rates are usually available. Many airlines offer fly/drive holidays to Munich, and the German Federal Railways promote a "Rail-and-Road" car-hire programme.

To hire a car, you'll need a valid driving licence held for at least half a year; the minimum age is 18. Normally a deposit is charged, but holders of major credit cards are exempt.

CIGARETTES, CIGARS, TOBACCO *(Zigaretten, Zigarren, Tabak)*. Foreign cigarette brands (manufactured under German licence) and a wide range of cigars and tobacco are sold in specialized tobacco shops, at kiosks and from vending machines. Most of the domestic makes resemble American cigarettes, but there are some with coarser tobacco.

As a rule, smoking is prohibited in theatres, cinemas, buses and trams. Trains have special smoking compartments.

A packet of …	**Eine Schachtel …**
A box of matches, please.	**Eine Schachtel Streichhölzer, bitte.**

CLOTHING. Munich's climate can go to extremes—from bitter-cold to hot and muggy. During the winter months, you'll need a heavy coat and warm clothing. In summer, lightweight garments are in order. Bring along a bathing suit, too, particularly if you want to take the sun in the English Garden—except, of course, for that restricted area by the river where you need nothing at all. A light wrap can come in handy on cool summer evenings. It may rain in spring and summer, so be prepared with a raincoat or umbrella.

At better hotels and restaurants, more formal clothes are expected, but there are few places where a tie is obligatory.

COMMUNICATIONS

Post offices. Munich's central post office stands just opposite the main railway station, on Bahnhofplatz 1. It remains open 24 hours a day to deal with mail, telegrams and telephone calls. A fax and telex service and currency exchange desk operate from 7 a.m. to 11 p.m. (and they also have write-read phones for deaf people).

Branch offices of Germany's Bundespost are generally open from **109**

C 8.30 a.m. to 6 p.m., Monday to Friday (till noon on Saturdays). They also handle telegrams and telephone calls.

Mail boxes are painted yellow with a black post-horn. Stamps can be purchased at yellow vending machines near mail boxes and at some tobacconists and stationers.

Poste restante (general delivery). This service is taken care of by Munich's central post office: if you have mail addressed to you c/o *Hauptpostlagernd*, it will automatically arrive at the central post office. Be sure to take your passport or identity card when you go to collect your mail.

Telegrams. Go in person to a post office or phone in messages from your hotel or any private telephone (dial 1131).

Telephone. Telephone booths, glass boxes with yellow frames, bear a sign showing a black receiver in a yellow square (national calls) or a green square (national and international calls). Area code numbers are listed in a special telephone book. Communications within Germany and to neighbouring countries are cheaper from 6 p.m. to 8 a.m. weekdays and all day Saturdays, Sundays and public holidays. Calls placed by hotels and restaurants generally carry a considerable surcharge.

Some useful numbers:

Enquiries: domestic 11 88, international 00 11 18
Operator: domestic 010, international 00 10

A stamp for this letter/postcard, please.	**Eine Briefmarke für diesen Brief/ diese Karte, bitte.**
express (special delivery)	**Eilzustellung**
airmail	**Luftpost**
registered	**Eingeschrieben**
Have you received any mail for ...?	**Ist Post da für ...?**
I want to send a telegram to ...	**Ich möchte ein Telegramm nach ... aufgeben.**
Can I use the telephone?	**Kann ich das Telefon benutzen?**
Can you get me this number in ...	**Können Sie mich mit dieser Nummer in ... verbinden?**
reverse-charge (collect) call	**R-Gespräch**
personal (person-to-person) call	**Gespräch mit Voranmeldung**

COMPLAINTS. If something goes wrong that you cannot take care of yourself, report the matter to the Munich tourist office.

In hotels and restaurants, discuss any problems with the proprietor or manager. If you fail to obtain satisfaction on the spot, contact the Bayerischer Hotel- und Gaststättenverband:

Türkenstrasse 7; tel. 23 68 050

Department stores provide a special counter *(Kundendienst)* to deal with customers' complaints.

If you have a problem with taxi service, call 77 30 77.

CONSULATES *(Konsulat)*

Canada	Tal 29, Munich 2; tel. 22 26 61
Eire	Mauerkircherstrasse 1a, Munich 80; tel. 98 57 23/25
South Africa	Sendlinger-Tor-Platz 5, Munich 2; tel. 260 50 81
United Kingdom	Amalienstrasse 62, Munich 40; tel. 381 62 80
U.S.A.	Königinstrasse 5, Munich 22; tel. 2 88 81

CRIME and THEFT. Compared to most urban centres, Munich's crime rate is quite low. Nonetheless it's advisable to take all the normal precautions. Don't leave money or valuables in your car or hotel room. Lock them in the hotel safe instead. If you are robbed, report the incident to the hotel receptionist and the nearest police station. The police will provide you with a certificate to present to your insurance company, or to your consulate if your passport has been stolen.

I want to report a theft.	**Ich möchte einen Diebstahl melden.**
My handbag/wallet/my passport has been stolen.	**Meine Handtasche/Brieftasche/ mein Pass ist gestohlen worden.**

CUSTOMS *(Zoll)* **and ENTRY REGULATIONS.** For a stay of up to three months, a valid passport is sufficient for citizens of Australia, Canada, New Zealand, South Africa and U.S.A. Visitors from Eire and the United Kingdom need only an identity card to enter West Germany.

The chart on p. 112 shows what you can take into West Germany duty free and, when returning home, into your own country:

111

C

Entering Germany from:	Cigarettes	Cigars	Tobacco	Spirits	Wine
1)	200 or	50 or	250 g.	1 l. and 2 l.	
2)	800 or	200 or	1 kg.	10 l. and 90 l.	
3)	400 or	100 or	500 g.	1 l. and 2 l.	
Into:					
Canada	200 and	50 and	900 g.	1.1 l. or 1.1 l.	
Eire } U.K. }	as 1) and 2) above				
U.S.A.	200 and	100 and	4)	1 l. or 1 l.	

1) EEC countries with goods bought tax free, and other European countries
2) EEC countries with goods not bought tax free
3) countries outside Europe
4) a reasonable quantity

Currency restrictions. There are no restrictions on the import or export of marks or any other currency.

I've nothing to declare.	**Ich habe nichts zu verzollen.**
It's for personal use.	**Es ist für meinen persönlichen Gebrauch.**

D **DRIVING.** To bring your car into Germany you will need:
- a national (or international for those coming from the U.S.A., Australia, South Africa) driving licence
- car registration papers
- a national identity sticker for your car and a red warning triangle in case of breakdown, as well as a first-aid kit containing rubber gloves and a mouth-protection mask

Insurance. Third-party insurance is compulsory. Visitors from abroad, except those from EEC and certain other European countries, will have to present their international insurance certificate (Green Card) or take out third-party insurance at the German border. Seat belts are obligatory, and that includes back-seat passengers if the car is so equipped. If you don't wear them, insurance companies reduce compensation in the event of an accident.

Driving conditions. Traffic jams, lack of parking space, pedestrian areas and one-way streets make driving in Munich a frustrating experience. It's better by far to get around town by public transport—the tourist office provides a brochure listing points of interest and detailing how to get there by bus or underground. Bear in mind that bottlenecks form on major approach roads into Munich at the beginning and end of peak holiday periods.

Drive on the right, pass on the left. Traffic in Germany follows the same basic rules that apply in most countries, though some may differ:

- on the Autobahn (motorway, expressway): 1) passing another vehicle on the right is prohibited; 2) cars with caravans (trailers) are not allowed to overtake on certain stretches (watch for signs); 3) should police or emergency vehicles need to pass through a traffic jam *(Stau)*, cars in the right lane must keep close to the right, and those in the left lane close to the left, thereby opening a passageway down the middle.

- in the absence of traffic lights, stop or yield signs, vehicles coming from the right have priority at intersections, unless otherwise indicated

- at roundabouts (traffic circles), approaching cars must give way to traffic already in mid-stream, unless otherwise indicated

- trams must be passed on the right and never at a stop (unless there's a traffic island)

- at dusk, and in case of bad visibility, headlights or dipped headlights must be used; driving with parking lights only is forbidden, even in built-up areas

Speed limits. The speed limit is 100 kilometres per hour (62 mph) on all open roads except for motorways and dual carriageways (divided highways), where there's no limit unless otherwise indicated (the suggested maximum speed is 130 kph, or 81 mph). In town, speed is restricted to 50 kph (31 mph), although in some areas this is reduced to 30 kph (18 mph). Cars towing caravans may not exceed 80 kph (50 mph).

Traffic police (see also POLICE) may confiscate the car keys of persons they consider unfit to drive. Drinking and driving, for example, is a very serious offence in Germany. The permissible level of alcohol in the blood is 0.8 per mille (millilitres), or about two glasses of beer. Be careful, too, to stay within speed limits; the police are getting more and more strict, and radar is used both inside and out of towns.

113

D **Breakdowns.** In the event of a breakdown on the Autobahn and other important roads, use one of the emergency telephones located every second kilometre (the nearest one is indicated by a small arrow on the reflector poles at the roadside). Ask for *Strassenwacht*, a service run jointly by the German automobile clubs ADAC *(Allgemeiner Deutscher Automobil Club)* and AvD *(Automobilclub von Deutschland)*. Assistance is free; towing and spare parts have to be paid for.

For round-the-clock breakdown service, call 19211.

Fuel and oil *(Benzin; Öl)*. You'll find service stations everywhere, many of them self-service. It's customary to tip attendants for any extra attention.

Fluid measures

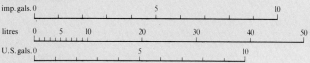

Road signs. Most road signs employed in Germany are international pictographs, but here are some written ones you might come across:

Einbahnstrasse	One-way street
Einordnen	Get into lane
Fussgänger	Pedestrians
Kurzparkzone	Short-term parking
Links fahren	Keep left
Parken verboten	No parking
Schlechte Fahrbahn	Poor road surface
Strassenarbeiten	Road works (Men working)
Umleitung	Diversion (Detour)
Vorsicht	Caution

(International) Driving Licence	**(Internationaler) Führerschein**
Car Registration Papers	**Kraftfahrzeugpapiere**
Green Card	**Grüne Karte**
Where's the nearest car park?	**Wo ist der nächste Parkplatz?**
Full tank, please.	**Bitte volltanken.**
Check the oil/tires/battery, please.	**Kontrollieren Sie bitte das Öl/ die Reifen/die Batterie.**
I've had a breakdown.	**Ich habe eine Panne.**
There's been an accident.	**Es ist ein Unfall passiert.**

114

ELECTRIC CURRENT. Germany has 220-volt, 50-cycle AC. Plugs are the standard continental type, for which British and North American appliances need an adaptor.

EMERGENCIES. See also under CONSULATES, DRIVING, HEALTH AND MEDICAL CARE OR POLICE according to the type of emergency.

Emergency telephone numbers:

Police	110
Fire	112
Ambulance	1 92 22

If you don't speak German, try English, or ask the first person you see to help you call.

Please, can you place an emergency call for me to the …?	**Würden Sie bitte … für mich anrufen?**
police/fire brigade/hospital	**die Polizei/die Feuerwehr/ das Krankenhaus**

GUIDES and TOURS. The tourist office will put you in touch with qualified guides and interpreters if you want a personally conducted tour or need linguistic assistance.

City sightseeing tours by bus start from opposite the main entrance of the central railway station, in front of the Hertie department store. Choose from the variety of different tours on offer, according to your interests. Daily excursions by coach to outlying towns and villages are also organized; enquire at the tourist office for details.

HAIRDRESSERS *(Damenfriseur)* and **BARBERS** *(Herrenfriseur).* Munich is well supplied with hairdressing establishments. Prices rise to *haute coiffure* levels in elegant Maximilianstrasse or trendy Schwabing; elsewhere in the city, salons are more likely to be moderate. Rates are often displayed in the window. Most establishments close on Saturday afternoons and all day Monday. It's always a good idea to telephone in advance for an appointment. You should tip 10 to 15%.

I'd like a shampoo and set.	**Waschen und Legen, bitte.**
haircut	**Schneiden**
shave	**Rasieren**
blow-dry (brushing)	**mit dem Fön trocknen**
Don't cut it too short.	**Schneiden Sie es nicht zu kurz.**
A little more off (here).	**(Hier) etwas kürzer.**

H **HEALTH and MEDICAL CARE.** Ask your insurance company before leaving home if you are covered for medical treatment in Germany. Visitors who are not reimbursed for medical bills abroad can take out a short-term holiday policy before setting out. Citizens of European Community countries may use the German Health Services for medical treatment. Ask for a copy of the requisite form at your local Health and Social Security Office.

In the event of accident or serious illness, call for an ambulance (19 222) or ask the medical emergency service staff (tel. 55 86 61) to recommend a competent doctor. You can also contact the American or British consulates for a list of English-speaking doctors and dentists.

It is perfectly safe to drink the tap water in Germany; only rarely will you see the sign "Kein Trinkwasser" (usually at public squares and in trains).

Pharmacies are open during normal shopping hours. At night and on Sundays and holidays, all chemists display the address of the nearest one open.

Where's the nearest (all-night) pharmacy?	**Wo ist die nächste diensthabende Apotheke?**
I need a doctor/dentist.	**Ich brauche einen Arzt/Zahnarzt.**
I have a pain here.	**Ich habe hier Schmerzen.**
stomach ache	**Magenschmerzen**
headache	**Kopfschmerzen**
a fever	**Fieber**
medical emergency service	**Ärztlicher Notdienst**
ambulance	**Rettungsdienst**
hospital	**Krankenhaus**

HITCH-HIKING. There are no laws or regulations prohibiting hitch-hiking, but there's little to encourage it: you'll be lucky if anyone stops for you. In Bavaria, it is permitted to thumb rides at the entrance of access roads to the Autobahn. However, it is strictly forbidden on the Autobahn itself.

(Student-) associations arrange inter-city trips *(Mitfahrgelegenheiten);* try the following addresses: Mitfahrzentrale, Lämmerstr. 4 (close to the main railway station), tel. 59 45 61; "Känguruh", Amalienstr. 87, tel. 28 01 24; Mitfahrcenter, Klenzestr. 57b, tel. 201 46 90; Mitfahrcenter (only for women), Klenzestr. 57b, tel. 2016510. There are fixed-price tickets for the journeys, according to the distance. And for a small fee, you can also have insurance cover.

HOURS. See also under COMMUNICATIONS and MONEY MATTERS.

Museum hours vary, but are usually from 9 a.m. to 4.30 or 5 p.m. Most museums close on Mondays. For exact time-tables, consult the official *Monatsprogramm* or enquire at the tourist office.

Restaurant meals. Breakfast is served until 10 a.m., lunch from noon to 2.30 p.m. and dinner from 6 to 11 p.m. In the city centre, most restaurants stay open all day.

Shops are generally open from 8.30 or 9 a.m. to 6.30 p.m., Monday to Friday, till 2 p.m. (some only till 12.30) on Saturdays (until 6 p.m. on the first Saturday of the month). On Thurdays, shops are open till 8.30 p.m. Shops outside the city centre usually close between 1 and 3 p.m.

Tourist information offices. The airport office operates from 8.30 a.m. to 10 p.m., Monday to Saturday, and from 1 to 9 p.m. on Sundays. The DB-Reisezentrum office in the central railway station opens daily from 8 a.m. to 11 p.m.

LANGUAGE. About one-third of the Munich population speak some form of Bavarian dialect. Real Bavarian is difficult to understand, even for the many northern Germans who live in Munich; but Bavarians can often be persuaded to speak something closer to High ("normal") German. English is widely understood and spoken, but don't take it for granted. Most of the larger shops, however, have English-speaking staff.

When entering a shop, it's customary to say *Guten Tag* (Good Day) or *Grüss Gott* ("God greet you"), the latter being widely used in Bavaria. When leaving, say *Auf Wiedersehen* (Good-bye); the less formal *Servus,* meaning "Bye" or "See you soon", is used among friends.

The Berlitz phrase book GERMAN FOR TRAVELLERS covers most of the situations you are likely to encounter in Germany, and the German-English/English-German pocket dictionary contains a special menu-reader supplement.

Do you speak English?   **Sprechen Sie Englisch?**

LAUNDRY and DRY-CLEANING. Having your laundry washed or cleaned by the hotel is of course the quickest and most convenient method, but prices are correspondingly high; it is therefore worth seeking out a laundromat *(Waschsalon)* or neighbourhood dry-clean-

L

ers. Dry-cleaning usually takes two days. Some cleaners offer a quick-service *(Schnellreinigung)* which takes a minimum of two hours and is slightly more expensive.

LOST PROPERTY. Munich's general lost-property office *(Fundbüro)* is at Ruppertstrasse 19 (tel. 23 31).

For property lost on trains, contact the Fundbüro at the central railway station, opposite Platform 26 (tel. 128 66 64), if it is within three days of the loss. Otherwise, contact the main lost-property offices of the Bundesbahn, at Landsbergerstr. 472; tel. 128 58 59. The S-Bahn lost-property office is at the east railway station *(Ostbahnhof)*, tel. 12 88 44 09.

For anything lost in a post office or telephone call box, enquire at the post office, Arnulfstrasse 195 (tel. 126 25 52).

For property lost at or near the airport, call 92 110.

| I've lost my wallet/my bag/ my passport. | **Ich habe meine Brieftasche/meine Tasche/meinen Pass verloren.** |

M

MAPS. Excellent free maps of Munich are available at the tourist offices, car-hire firms and bigger hotels. Falk-Verlag, Hamburg, who prepared the maps for this book, publish a detailed map of the city. For the hiker, there is a series called *Kompass Wanderkarten*—on sale in most bookstores—that will keep you on the right track as you wander through Bavaria.

| I'd like a street plan of Munich. | **Ich möchte einen Stadtplan von München.** |
| a road map/hiking map of this region | **eine Strassenkarte/Wanderkarte dieser Gegend** |

MEETING PEOPLE. Bavarians are at their most relaxed in traditional taverns and beer gardens. Just take a place at one of the long tables for a meal or a glass of beer, and you'll soon find yourself chatting to new acquaintances. One of the most popular meeting places in Munich itself is the beer garden at the Chinese Tower in the English Garden. Activity here reaches fever pitch on summer weekends. Students have long been attracted to the Schwabing district with its cafés, bars and restaurants. You'll also find lively open-air cafés around Marienplatz, which has been transformed into a pedestrian zone. And then, of course, there are the two great Bavarian festivals, Fasching and the Oktoberfest, both of which provide plenty of opportunities for celebrating with local people from all walks of life.

MONEY MATTERS

Currency. Germany's monetary unit is the *Deutsche Mark (DM)*. The mark is divided into 100 *Pfennig (Pf.)*.

   Coins: 1, 2, 5, 10 and 50 Pf. and DM 1, 2, 5 and 10.

   Notes: DM 5, 10, 20, 50, 100, 200, 500 and 1,000.

Banking hours are usually from 8.15 a.m. to 12.30 p.m. and 1.45 to 3.30 p.m., Monday to Friday (Thursday until 5.30 p.m.). Some bigger banks in the city centre remain open during the lunch hour. Banks at the airport operate daily from 7 or 7.30 a.m. till around 9 p.m. Banking transactions can also be made at the central railway station from 6 a.m. to 11 p.m. every day.

Changing money. Foreign currency can be changed at ordinary banks *(Bank)*, savings banks *(Sparkasse)* and currency exchange offices *(Wechselstube)*. It can also be done at hotels, travel agencies and Munich's central post office, but rates are not as good.

Credit cards, traveller's cheques, eurocheques. Traveller's cheques are welcome almost everywhere, and most major hotels and many restaurants and shops accept credit cards. Eurocheques are widely used in Germany.

I want to change some pounds/dollars.	**Ich möchte Pfund/Dollars wechseln.**
Do you accept traveller's cheques?	**Nehmen Sie Reiseschecks?**
Can I pay with this credit card?	**Kann ich mit dieser Kreditkarte zahlen?**

NEWSPAPERS and MAGAZINES *(Zeitung; Zeitschrift)*. Major British, American and continental newspapers and magazines are on sale

at newsagents in the city centre, as well as at larger hotels, the central railway station and airport.

   A guide to forthcoming events *(Monatsprogramm)*, published each month, is available at the tourist office, at hotels and news-stands.

   There is an English bookshop with a large selection of English paperbacks in Schellingstrasse, near the university. Other sources of English-language books and newspapers are the:

British Council Library, Rosenheimerstr. 116b (Haus 93—near the Ostbahnhof railway station); tel. 40 18 32

Amerika Haus Library, Karolinenplatz 3; tel. 59 53 67/68

Have you any English-language newspapers?	**Haben Sie Zeitungen in englischer Sprache?**

PHOTOGRAPHY. Some of the world's best cameras come from Germany, so you might even think of getting equipped here. All brands of film are easily found. Developing usually takes 1–2 days, but some shops provide overnight service.

Some airport security machines use X-rays which can ruin your film. Ask that it be hand-checked, or enclose it in a lead-lined bag.

I'd like a roll of film for this camera.	**Ich hätte gern einen Film für diesen Apparat.**
black-and-white film	**Schwarzweissfilm**
colour prints	**Farbfilm**
colour slides	**Diafilm**
How long will it take to develop this film?	**Wie lange dauert das Entwickeln?**
May I take a picture (of you)?	**Darf ich (Sie) fotografieren?**

POLICE *(Polizei).* Germany's police wear green uniforms. You'll see them on white motorcycles or in green-and-white cars.

Street parking in towns is supervised by police officers in dark-blue uniforms. If you are fined, they have the right to ask you to pay on the spot.

The police emergency number is 110.

Munich's central police station *(Polizeipräsidium)* is at Ettstrasse 2.

Where's the nearest police station? **Wo ist die nächste Polizeiwache?**

PUBLIC HOLIDAYS *(Feiertag).* The chart below shows the public holidays celebrated in Bavaria, when shops, banks, official departments and many restaurants are closed. If a holiday falls on a Thursday, many people make it into a long weekend.

On December 24 and 31, shops stay open till midday. Most restaurants, theatres, cinemas and concert halls close on Christmas Eve.

Jan. 1	*Neujahr*	New Year's Day
Jan. 6	*Heilige Drei Könige*	Epiphany
May 1	*Tag der Arbeit*	Labour Day
Aug. 15	*Mariä Himmelfahrt*	Assumption Day
Oct. 3	*Tag der Deutschen Einheit*	Day of National Unity
Nov. 1	*Allerheiligen*	All Saints' Day
Dec. 25, 26	*Weihnachten*	Christmas

Movable dates:	Karfreitag	Good Friday
	Ostermontag	Easter Monday
	Christi Himmelfahrt	Ascension Day
	Pfingstmontag	Whit Monday
	Fronleichnam	Corpus Christi
	Buss- und Bettag	Day of Prayer and
	(3rd Wed. in Nov.)	Repentance

RADIO and TV *(Radio; Fernsehen)*. You can easily pick up the BBC World Service, American Forces Network (AFN) or the Voice of America anywhere in Germany. Shortwave reception is excellent, especially at night. The Bavarian Radio Service *(Bayerischer Rundfunk)* broadcasts the news in English every day. As for television, there are two national channels—ARD (Channel One) and ZDF (Channel Two)—plus a regional station called *Drittes Programm*, affiliated with the Bayerische Rundfunk. Films are sometimes shown in the original English version, and a news bulletin is relayed in English once a week.

RELIGIOUS SERVICES. Almost half of the Munich population are Roman Catholic and about one-third Protestant. There is also a large Jewish community.

Several church services are held in English for different denominations, such as: St. Bonifaz, Karlstrasse, and in Kreuzkirche, Kreuzstrasse (Roman Catholic) and Seybothstrasse 4 (Anglican-Episcopal). For times of these—and other—services, refer to the monthly guide *Monatsprogramm*.

TIME DIFFERENCES. Germany follows Central European Time (GMT + 1). In summer, the clock is put one hour ahead (GMT + 2):

New York	London	**Munich**	Jo'burg	Sydney	Auckland
6 a.m.	11 a.m.	**noon**	noon	8 p.m.	10 p.m.

What time is it, please? **Wie spät ist es, bitte?**

TIPPING. Since a service charge is normally included in hotel and restaurant bills, tipping is not obligatory but is widely practised. It's appropriate to give something extra to bellboys, hat-check attendants, etc., for their services. The chart on p. 122 makes some suggestions as to how much to leave.

121

Porter, per bag	DM 1–2
Maid, per week	DM 5–10
Lavatory attendant	DM 0.50–1
Waiter	optional (round off)
Taxi driver	round off
Hairdresser/Barber	10–15%
Tourist guide	10%

TOILETS. Public toilets are easily found: museums, all restaurants, bars, cafés, large stores, airports and railway stations provide facilities. If there's an attendant, and hand towels and soap are offered, you should leave a small tip. Always have several 10-Pfennig coins ready in case the door has a slot machine.

Toilets may be labelled with symbols of a man or a woman or the initials *W. C.* Otherwise *Herren* (Gentlemen) and *Damen* (Ladies) or a double zero (00) sign are indicated.

Where are the toilets, please?   **Wo sind die Toiletten, bitte?**

TOURIST INFORMATION OFFICES. The German National Tourist Board—Deutsche Zentrale für Tourismus e.V. (DZT)—can inform you about when to go, where to stay and what to see in Munich. Headquarters is at:

Beethovenstrasse 69, D-6000 Frankfurt am Main: tel (069) 7 57 20

The national tourist organization also maintains offices in many countries throughout the world:

Canada   1290 Bay Street, Toronto, Ont. M5R 2C3; tel. (416) 968-1570
                    P.O. Box 417, 2 Fundy, Place Bonaventure, Montreal, Que. H5A 1B8; tel. (514) 878-9885

United Kingdom 61, Conduit Street, London WIR OEN; tel. (01) 734-2600

U.S.A.   747 Third Avenue, 33rd floor, New York, NY 10017; tel. (212) 308-3300
                    Broadway Plaza, Suite 2230, 444 South Flower Street, Los Angeles, CA 90071; tel. (213) 688-7332

Munich's tourist offices are situated in the arrival hall of the airport and near the Bayerstrasse exit of the central railway station. Address enquiries to:

Fremdenverkehrsamt München, Postfach, 8000 Munich 1;
tel. (089) 2 39 11; fax 239 13 13

In addition to providing free maps, lists and brochures, Munich's tourist offices offer a hotel booking service for a small fee. The official *Monatsprogramm* of events (concerts, theatre, exhibitions) is on sale there, as are the 24-hour tickets for unlimited trips by tram, bus, U-Bahn and S-Bahn.

You can also listen to recorded tourist information in English:

Museums, galleries	23 91 62
Palaces and other sights	23 91 72

For information about Upper Bavaria, contact the Munich-Upper Bavaria Tourist Association at the following address:

Fremdenverkehrsverband München-Oberbayern, Sonnenstrasse 10/III, 8000 Munich 2; tel. (089) 59 73 47/48; fax 59 31 87.

TRANSPORT. Munich is served by an efficient network of **buses, trams, U-Bahn** (underground railway) and **S-Bahn** (suburban railway, a part of the German Federal Railways). Both the U- and S-Bahn cross the city centre in all directions, while the S-Bahn goes out to suburbs and the surrounding countryside. All forms of public transport operate from about 5 a.m. to 1 a.m. daily. Free maps and information are available at the tourist offices.

Tickets are interchangeable between U-Bahn, S-Bahn, buses and trams, and entitle you to free transfers for up to two hours so long as you travel in the same direction. Buy your tickets from the big blue vending machines at U- and S-Bahn stations (or on buses and at tram stops, tobacconists, newsagents and stationers that display a white "K"). Be sure to cancel them in the blue cancelling machines positioned at platform entrances and in buses and trams. Vending machines are marked *Einzelfahrkarte* (single ticket) or *Streifenkarte* (strip ticket). Munich Transport *(Münchner Verkehrs-Verbund—MVV)* also offer reduced-price 24-hour tickets which can be used throughout the metropolitan area. They are sold by machines marked *24-Stunden-Karte* and at the tourist offices.

Taxis. Munich taxis are beige in colour. Catch one at a rank, or hail a driver roaming the streets. There never seem to be enough taxis at **123**

T rush hour, so it would be wise to book in advance if you can, either through your hotel receptionist or by phoning 2161-0 or 19410.

Inter-city bus services. Rural areas are served by the Federal Railways *(Bundesbahn)* buses and the Federal Post Office *(Bundespost)* buses, as well as by local companies. Bus terminals are invariably close to a railway station, and there you'll find information about routes and fares.

In Munich, the bus terminal is in Arnulfstrasse, in the front of Starnberg Station (on the north side of the central railway station).

Trains. Deutsche Bundesbahn (DB) trains are extremely comfortable and fast, as well as punctual. They are classified thus:

ICE *(Inter-City Express)*	High speed trains (280 km/h) between Munich and Hamburg via Würzburg–Nuremburg or Frankfurt–Stuttgart. First and second class with high degree of comfort; with supplement
EC *(Euro-City)*	International trains; with supplement; first and second class
IC *(Inter-City)*	Regular long-distance trains; between major cities; first and second class; with supplement
FD *(Fern-Express)*	Intermediate- to long-distance trains; with supplement on journeys of less than 50 kilometres
D *(Schnellzug)*	Intermediate- to long-distance trains
E *(Eilzug)*	Trains making local stops
Nahverkehrszug	Local trains, stop at all stations

Tickets for distance of up to 100 kilometres are valid for a day, return tickets for longer journeys for a month, and return tickets to destinations abroad for two months. A number of special reduced-price offers and bargain tickets are available:

European Money-Spinner Fares offer return (round-trip) journeys from the U.K. to ten destinations within Germany at about 25% off.

DB Tourist Cards for foreign visitors only. Bring along your passport when ordering. The holder can travel for four, nine or 16 consecutive days on the entire network of the Deutsche Bundesbahn. The card also includes coach and river-boat transport and free travel in Munich's suburban areas on the S-Bahn.

Eurailpasses are special rover tickets covering most of Western Europe. For non-European residents only, they can be purchased before leaving home or at railway stations in Germany.

Anyone under 26 can purchase an *Inter-Rail* card which allows one

month of unlimited 2nd-class rail travel on all participating European railways. The *Rail Europ S* card entitles senior citizens to buy train tickets for European destinations at reduced prices.

Tourenkarten, regional rail rover tickets for a given area are bought in Germany. They allow ten days' unlimited travel on regional rail services, with 50% reduction on buses; the only requirement is that your rail journey must have covered at least 250 kilometres one way *before* you can obtain it.

Children under 4 travel free, from 4 to 11 inclusive, half price.

DB Junior Passes entitle young people between 12 and 22 and students under 27 to unlimited travel at half-price on DB routes for one year.

For further details, ask for the brochure *Discover Germany by Rail* at travel agencies and DB railway offices.

When's the next bus/train to...?	**Wann fährt der nächste Bus/Zug nach...?**
I want a ticket to...	**Ich möchte eine Fahrkarte nach...**
single (one-way)	**einfach**
return (round-trip)	**hin und zurück**
first/second class	**erste/zweite Klasse**

SOME USEFUL EXPRESSIONS

yes/no	**ja/nein**
please/thank you	**bitte/danke**
excuse me/you're welcome	**Entschuldigung/gern geschehen**
how long/how far	**wie lange/wie weit**
where/when/how	**wo/wann/wie**
yesterday/today/tomorrow	**gestern/heute/morgen**
day/week/month/year	**Tag/Woche/Monat/Jahr**
cheap/expensive	**billig/teuer**
hot/cold	**heiss/kalt**
open/closed	**offen/geschlossen**
free (vacant)/occupied	**frei/besetzt**
I don't understand.	**Ich verstehe nicht.**
What does this mean?	**Was bedeutet das?**
Waiter/Waitress, please!	**Ober/Fräulein, bitte!**
How much is that?	**Wieviel kostet das?**

Index

An asterisk (*) next to a page number indicates a map reference.

U-Bahn and S-Bahn System

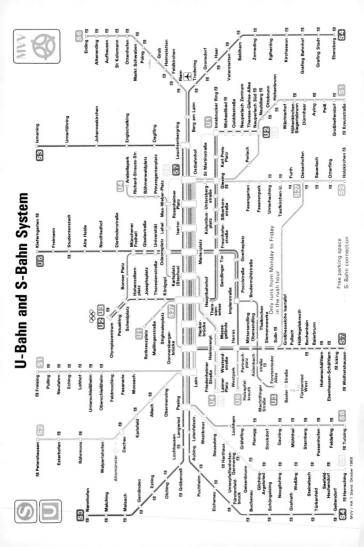

Free parking space
S-Bahn connection

Only runs from Monday to Friday in the rush hour

MVV / HA 1 Stand: Oktober 1989

Selection of Munich Hotels and Restaurants

Where do you start? Choosing a hotel or restaurant in a place you're not familiar with can be daunting.

Our own Berlitz criteria have been (a) price and (b) location. In the hotel section, for a double room with bath and breakfast, Higher-priced means above DM 270, Medium-priced DM 180–270, Lower-priced below DM 180. As to restaurants, for a meal consisting of a starter, a main course and a dessert, Higher-priced means above DM 70, Medium-priced DM 50–70, Lower-priced below DM 50. Special features (where applicable), plus regular closing days are also given. As a general rule many Munich hotels and restaurants close around Christmas and New Year and restaurants also often a couple of weeks in August. For hotels and restaurants, checking first to make certain that they are open and advance reservations are both advisable. In Munich, hotel and restaurant prices include service and taxes.

HOTELS

HIGHER-PRICED
(above DM 270)

Arabella-Westpark-Hotel
Garmischer Str. 2
München 2
Tel. 5 19 60; fax 5 19 66 49
258 rooms
Indoor swimming pool. Sauna.

Austrotel – München
Arnulfstr. 2
München 2
Tel. 5 38 60; fax 53 86 22 55
174 rooms
View over Munich from 15th-floor restaurant.

Budapest
Schwanthalerstr. 36
München 2
Tel. 55 11 10; fax 55 11 19 92
100 rooms

Continental
Max-Joseph-Str. 5
München 2
Tel. 55 15 70; fax 55 15 75 00
149 rooms
Outdoor dining.

Eden-Hotel-Wolff
Arnulfstr. 4
München 2
Tel. 55 11 50; fax 55 11 55 55
214 rooms

Königshof
Karlsplatz 25
München 2
Tel. 55 13 60; fax 55 13 61 13
106 rooms
Restaurant with notably good cuisine and outstanding wine list.

Hilton Park
Am Tucherpark 7
München 22
Tel. 3 84 50; fax 38 45 18 45
477 rooms
Outdoor dining. Beer garden. Sauna. Indoor swimming pool.

Vier Jahreszeiten Kempinski
Maximilianstr. 17
München 22
Tel. 23 03 90; fax 23 03 96 93
344 rooms
Quiet hotel. Sauna. Indoor swimming pool. Walterspiel restaurant (notably good cuisine).

MEDIUM-PRICED
(DM 180–270)

An der Oper
Falkenturmstr. 10
München 2
Tel. 2 90 02 70; fax 29 00 27 29
55 rooms
Bouillabaisse restaurant.

Ariston
Unsöldstr. 10
München 22
Tel. 22 26 91; fax 2 91 35 95
61 rooms
No restaurant.

3

Drei Löwen
Schillerstr. 8
München 2
Tel. 55 10 40; fax 55 10 49 05
130 rooms

Erzgießerei-Europe
Erzgießereistr. 15
München 2
Tel. 12 68 20; fax 1 23 61 98
106 rooms

Europäischer Hof
Bayerstr. 31
München 2
Tel. 55 15 10; fax 55 15 12 22
160 rooms
No restaurant.

Intercity-Hotel
Bahnhofplatz 2
München 2
Tel. 55 85 71; fax 59 62 29
209 rooms

Mercure
Senefelder Str. 9
München 2
Tel. 55 13 20; fax 59 64 44
167 rooms

Metropol
Bayerstr. 43
München 2
Tel. 53 07 64; fax 5 32 81 34
275 rooms

LOWER-PRICED
(below DM 180)

Apollo
Mittererstr. 7
München 2
Tel. 53 95 31; fax 53 40 33
74 rooms
No restaurant.

Blauer Bock
Sebastiansplatz 9
München 2
Tel. 23 17 80; fax 23 17 82 00
76 rooms
No restaurant.

Brack
Lindwurmstr. 153
München 2
Tel. 77 10 52; fax 7 25 06 15
50 rooms
No restaurant.

Stachus
Bayerstr. 7
München 2
Tel. 59 28 81; fax 5 23 21 33
65 rooms
No restaurant.

Uhland
Uhlandstr. 1
München 2
Tel. 53 92 77; fax 53 11 14
25 rooms
No restaurant.

GREATER MUNICH

HIGHER-PRICED
(above DM 270)

Arabella-Hotel
Arabellastr. 5
München 81-Bogenhausen
Tel. 9 23 20; fax 92 32 44 49
478 rooms
View of Munich. Massage. Sauna.
Indoor swimming pool.

Holiday Inn
Leopoldstr. 194
München 40-Schwabing
Tel. 38 17 90; fax 38 17 98 88
363 rooms
Massage. Sauna.
Indoor swimming pool.

Palace
Trogerstr. 21
München 80-Bogenhausen
Tel. 4 70 50 91; fax 4 70 50 90
73 rooms
Elegant decor. Sauna.

Preysing
Preysingstr. 1
München 80-Haidhausen
Tel. 48 10 11; fax 4 47 09 98
76 rooms
Sauna. Indoor swimming pool.

Prinzregent
Ismaninger Str. 42
München 80-Bogenhausen
Tel. 41 60 50; fax 41 60 54 66
68 rooms
Elegant, rustic decor. No restaurant.

Sheraton
Arabellastr. 6
München 81-Bogenhausen
Tel. 9 26 40; fax 91 68 77
650 rooms
View of Munich. Beer garden.
Massage. Sauna. Indoor swim-
ming pool. Garden.

MEDIUM-PRICED
(DM 180–270)

Arabella-Olympiapark-Hotel
Helene-Mayer-Ring 12
München 40-Schwabing
Tel. 3 51 60 71; fax 3 54 37 30
105 rooms
Outdoor dining. Free admission to
the indoor swimming pool at the
thermal springs.

Kent
Englschalkinger Str. 245
München 81-Englschalking
Tel. 93 50 73; fax 93 50 72
49 rooms
Sauna. No restaurant.

Königstein
Frankfurter Ring 28
München 40-Milbertshofen
Tel. 35 96 11; fax 3 59 78 80
42 rooms
No restaurant.

Orbis Hotel
Karl-Marx-Ring 87
München 83-Neu Perlach
Tel. 6 32 70; fax 6 32 74 07
185 rooms
Sauna. Indoor swimming pool.

LOWER-PRICED
(below DM 180)

Gästehaus Englischer Garten
Liebergesellstr. 8
München 40-Schwabing
Tel. 39 20 34
14 rooms
Quiet hotel. Garden. No restaurant.

Hotel und Gasthof Sollner Hof
Herterichstr. 63
München 71-Solln
Tel. 79 20 99; tlx. 5218264
25 rooms
Beer garden.

Kriemhild
Guntherstr. 16
München 19-Nymphenburg
Tel. 17 00 77
Fax 17 74 78
18 rooms
No restaurant.

Obermaier
Truderinger Str. 304B
München 82-Trudering
Tel. 42 90 21
Fax 42 64 00
30 rooms
No restaurant.

Petra
Marschnerstr. 73
München 60-Pasing
Tel. 83 20 41
18 rooms
Garden. No restaurant.

RESTAURANTS

HIGHER-PRICED
(above DM 70)

Aubergine
Maximiliansplatz 5
München 2
Tel. 59 81 71; fax 5 23 67 53
Superb cuisine. Closed Sunday and Monday. Reservation essential.

Boettner
Theatinerstr. 8
München 2
Tel. 22 12 10
Small old-Munich-style restaurant with notably good cuisine. Closed Saturday evening.

Le Gourmet im Weinhaus Schwarzwälder
Hartmannstr. 8
München 2
Tel. 2 12 09 58
Notably good cuisine. Closed Sunday and Monday.

Sabitzer
Reitmorstr. 21
München 22
Tel. 29 85 84; fax 3 00 33 04
Notably good cuisine. Dinner only on Saturday and Sunday.

MEDIUM-PRICED
(DM 50–70)

Austernkeller
Stollbergstr. 11
München 22
Tel. 29 87 87
Dinner only. Closed Monday. Reservation essential.

Csarda Piroschka
Prinzregentenstr. 1
München 22
Tel. 29 54 25; fax 29 38 50
*Hungarian restaurant with gypsy
music. Open from 6 p.m. Closed
Sunday.*

Gasthaus Glockenbach
Kapuzinerstr. 29
München 2
Tel. 53 40 43
*Formerly Bavarian beer hall.
Closed Sunday and Monday.*

La Piazzetta
Oskar-v.-Miller-Ring 3
München 3
Tel. 28 29 90
*Outdoor dining. Beer garden.
Modern Italian restaurant in
Florentine style. Dinner only on
Saturday.*

Mövenpick im Künstlerhaus
Lenbachplatz 8
München 2
Tel. 55 78 65; fax 5 23 65 38
Outdoor dining.

Spatenhaus-Bräustuben
Residenzstr. 12
München 2
Tel. 22 78 41; fax 29 40 76
*Outdoor dining. Alpine-country
decor.*

Zum Bürgerhaus
Pettenkoferstr. 1
München 2
Tel. 59 79 09
*Farmer-style furnishings. Court-
yard terrace. Closed Saturday
until 6 p.m. and Sunday.*

LOWER PRICED
(below DM 50)

Augustiner Gaststätten
Neuhauser Str. 16
München 2
Tel. 55 19 92 57
Beer garden.

Goldene Stadt
Oberanger 44
München 2
Tel. 26 43 82
*Bohemian specialities. Closed
Sunday.*

Hackerkeller und Schäfflerstuben
Theresienhöhe 4
München 2
Tel. 50 70 04; fax 50 17 21
Beer garden.

Pschorrkeller
Theresienhöhe 7
München 2
Tel. 50 10 88
Beer garden.

Spatenhofkeller
Neuhauser Str. 26
München 2
Tel. 26 40 10
Outdoor dining.

Zum Pschorrbräu
Neuhauser Str. 11
München 2
Tel. 2 60 30 01
Outdoor dining.

Zum Spöckmeier
Rosenstr. 9
München 2
Tel. 26 80 88
Outdoor dining. Closed Sunday.

GREATER MUNICH

HIGHER-PRICED

**Das kleine Restaurant
im Gasthof Böswirth**
Waidachanger 9
München 60-Langwied
Tel. 8 11 97 63
*Notably good cuisine. Dinner only.
Closed Sunday and Monday.
12 rooms.*

Käfer Schänke
Prinzregentenstr. 73
München 80-Bogenhausen
Tel. 4 16 80
*Outdoor dining. Rustic and period
furnishings. Closed Sunday.*

Preysing-Keller
Innere-Wiener-Str. 6
München 80-Haidhausen
Tel. 48 10 15
*Notably good cuisine. Exceptional
wine list. Vaults with rustic decor.
Dinner only. Closed Sunday.*

Tantris
Johann-Fichte-Str. 7
München 40-Schwabing
Tel. 36 20 61; fax 3 61 84 69
*Superb cuisine. Modern restau-
rant building with elegant decor.
Outdoor dining. Dinner only on
Monday and Saturday. Closed
Sunday. Reservation essential.*

MEDIUM-PRICED

da Pippo
Brahmsstr. 32
München 80-Bogenhausen
Tel. 4 70 48 48; fax 47 64 64
*Italian cuisine. Outdoor dining.
Closed Sunday.*

Passatore
Wasserburger Landstr. 212
München 82-Trudering
Tel. 4 30 30 00
*Italian cuisine. Outdoor dining.
Closed Wednesday.*

Restaurant 33
Feilitzschstr. 33
München 40-Schwabing
Tel. 34 25 28
Outdoor dining. Dinner only.

Romagna Antica
Elisabethstr. 52
München 40-Schwabing
Tel. 2 71 63 55; fax 2 71 13 64
*Italian cuisine. Outdoor dining.
Closed Sunday.*

Seehaus
Kleinhesselohe 3
München 40-Schwabing
Tel. 39 70 72; fax 34 18 03
View. Lakeside terrace.

LOWER-PRICED

Tai Tung
Prinzregentenstr. 60 (Villa Stuck)
München 80-Bogenhausen
Tel. 47 11 00
Chinese cuisine. Closed Monday.